5-1-97

TO MY good FRIEND "TED".
THIS BOOK REFLECTS OUR
ON
MUTUAL FEELINGS ON THE
WAY BASEBALL SHOULD BE.

AS EVER,

P.S. ALSO — AL KALINE FROM
BALTIMORE — MR. KETZER'S
FAVORITE PLAYER & PERSON.

John Fetzer: On a Handshake
The Times and Triumphs of
a Tiger Owner

Dan Ewald

SAGAMORE PUBLISHING
Champaign, IL 61820

Dustjacket design: Michelle R. Dressen
Book design, editor: Susan M. McKinney
Proofreader: Kathryn Meyer

ISBN:1-57167-127-7
Library of Congress Catalog Card Number: 97-66501

Printed in the United States.

*This book is dedicated to Jim Campbell, who showed
me the strength of honesty ...
to Bo Schembechler, who taught me the meaning of courage ...
and particularly to Sparky Anderson,
for friendship that knows no bounds.*

———————————————

Contents

Acknowledgments

T he author wishes to acknowledge all of the countless people and events that combined to weave this fabric of a particularly wonderful period of baseball history. In particular, special acknowledgment is accorded to: the Fetzer Institute for its dedication and vast array of historical resources; Lou Leeburg for his diligence; Bruce Fetzer for his careful insight; Scott Grimwood for his meticulous contributions of historical accuracy; the Detroit Tigers for their generous loan of historical materials; Mike Pearson and Susan McKinney for their commitment to editorial excellence; Connie Bell for all of her thankless and timely assistance in the gathering of historical matter; and Dan Ewald Jr. whose memories and insights into this baseball era that no longer exists provided the impetus to complete the project.

John Earl Fetzer
March 25, 1901 – February 20, 1991

PROFESSIONAL BASEBALL HIGHLIGHTS

1956   Organized 11-man syndicate to purchase Detroit Baseball Company from estate of W.O. Briggs; became one-third owner and Chairman of the Board.

1960   Became two-thirds owner and President of Detroit Baseball Company.

1962   Became sole owner, Chairman and President of Detroit Baseball Club.

1962   Detroit Tigers baseball tour of Japan, Okinawa and Korea under auspices of U.S. State Department.

1963-71
        Chairman of Major League Baseball Television Committee.

1968   Detroit Tigers become World Champions.

1968   Received from the state of Michigan awards from the Governor and legislative bodies.

1977   Sold Tiger Stadium to City of Detroit for $1 in return for 30-year lease.

1977   Received the Summit Award from the Greater Detroit Chamber of Commerce for Community Service.

1981   Received the August A. Busch Jr. Award for meritorious service to baseball. Award is given only occasionally and for extraordinary achievements.

1981   Bud Selig, owner of the Milwaukee Brewers and later Acting Commissioner creates the John E. Fetzer Award for meritorious service to baseball.

1981   Elected Honorary Vice President of the American League.

1983   Sold Detroit Baseball Club to Thomas S. Monaghan; continued as Chairman of the Board and stockholder.

1984   Inducted into Michigan Sports Hall of Fame.

1984   Received the rarely given Commissioner of Baseball's Excellence Award.

1984   Detroit Tigers become World Champions.

1984   Receives a U.S. Congressional Record Citation.

1985   Honored with State of Michigan Humanitarian Award of the Year.

1989   Becomes Chairman Emeritus of the Detroit Tigers Baseball Club Board of Directors.

1989   Fetzer/Yawkey wing of Baseball's Hall of Fame commissioned in Cooperstown.

MAJOR LEAGUES BASEBALL
COMMITTEES MEMBERSHIP

1960-65, 1973, 1975-79 Member, Major League Executive Council.

1963-
64   Member, Major League Pension Committee.

1965   Member, Board of Directors of the American League.

1967   Chairman, American League Radio-Television Committee.

1973   Chairman, American League Planning Committee.

Foreword

I was just a kid when John Fetzer and a group of investors bought the Detroit Tigers in 1956. I had won the American League batting title the year before. All I cared about was playing baseball. At the time, it didn't really matter to me who owned the team.

As time went on and I became more established in Detroit, I realized how much ownership of the Tigers meant. Not just to me, but to the entire community. In fact, to the whole state of Michigan.

The Tigers are a true baseball tradition. And that's the way Mr. Fetzer always treated the franchise. He respected baseball history and always defended the integrity of the game.

He always said he really never owned the Tigers; he was only their guardian. The team belonged to Tiger fans everywhere. He was the protector of their hopes and dreams.

He believed the Tigers were a team for the working-class people. As long as he was involved, they would always remain in Detroit.

Mr. Fetzer was not a very public figure. He protected his privacy. Quietly behind the scenes, though, he was one of the most powerful people in the game.

Mr. Fetzer cared about the Tigers. He cared about baseball and he cared about Detroit. I'm proud to have spent almost my entire career playing for him. I'm delighted that this book has been written to finally give some credit, which has been long overdue.

— Al Kaline

Introduction

Growing up on the near west side of Detroit, I used to walk to the ball park. It was called Briggs Stadium back then in the '50s. One short block to West Grand Boulevard. A few short blocks around the Boulevard's left and right elbow curves. Then a glorious stroll down Michigan Avenue's parade of pawn shops, taverns and open-air ethnic markets.

Michigan Avenue itself was a ribbon of rustic red brick. An electric-powered streetcar sliced its middle. There was a rainbow of colors. In the humid summer months, the smell from the meat-packing slaughter houses hung over the neighborhood like an invisible cloud. On particularly sticky days, kids promised themselves never to eat bacon again.

Foot traffic was always brisk. Today's fears of walking downtown never entered anyone's mind. There was no sense of danger. The old men on the streets—hobos and bums to the uninitiated— were too busy bouncing from bar to bar or bargaining with a pawn shop owner to cause any problems.

The business section was always humming with all the sounds and smells common to every American big city downtown. Office workers scurried around the narrow streets and tall buildings. The Penobscot Building, with its flashing red light as a crown, stood majestically as the king of all Detroit skyscrapers.

Shoppers darted in and out of a maze of department and specialty stores. Hudson's, with its 12 stories of merchandise, ruled the Woodward Avenue retail section. There were other giants like Crowley's and Kern's. But a shopping spree was not complete without a visit to Hudson's. No kid growing up in Detroit failed to visit Hudson's famous 12th floor some time during the Christmas season. That was Toyland. It provided a comfortable oasis for waiting out the winter until baseball returned in the spring.

Theaters sprinkled the entire downtown area. There was the Michigan. The Palms. The United Artists. The Fox. The Adams. The Broadway Capitol.These were not the usual neighborhood theaters. These were royally constructed monuments featuring European fixtures of decor.

On the edges of downtown stood live burlesque theaters. Kids, of course, were not allowed. But all the boys would look at the marquees and stare at the pictures, only imagining what really went on inside.

Downtown back then was something like Alice's Restaurant. Anything you wanted was there. There was something for everyone. People were everywhere. It was the heart of the city.

Nothing, though, matched that walk to the ballpark that sat proudly on the western edge of downtown. It didn't matter where the Tigers stood in the standings. Each walk was better than the newest ride at the downriver Bob-Lo Island Amusement Park. That's because each walk ended at the prettiest park on the planet.

On spring afternoons, the nuns who provided my first taste of formal education had a pretty good idea of my whereabouts when I was absent from class. I spent a few late hours after school in detention making up missed arithmetic and reading assignments. It was a fair price to pay for an afternoon at the park.

My addiction to baseball struck early. My appetite for playing baseball from sun up to sun down daily throughout the summer in the alleys, streets and parking lots around the neighborhood was insatiable. I was captured by the romance of the Detroit Tigers.

Al Kaline won a batting title when he was only 20 in 1955. I didn't think anybody in the world was a greater hero than Kaline. Not Mickey Mantle. Not Ted Williams. Not Willie Mays. Certainly not any of those National Football League stars. In my rating system of sports heroes, they finished far down the list behind even the lowliest Tiger benchwarmer like Jim Brideweser.

Kaline was a sculptured slice of elegance in a game of good old-fashioned hardball. He robbed hitters of extra bases by digging into the rightfield corner. He snatched wicked line drives before they could whistle over the fence. He knew when to gamble on taking an extra base and when to play it safe. Nobody was deadlier at the plate in a clutch situation. He made all these things look easier than my walk to the park. I remember wondering if he could actually control his sweat.

Kaline was the uncrowned prince of Detroit sports in those days. And he was surrounded by plenty of support. In fact, anyone who wore the Tiger uniform seemed bigger than life back then.

That was the way it was in Detroit. New York had Mantle. Boston had Williams. St. Louis had Stan "The Man" Musial. There were plenty of heroes to go around. Baseball was king. No one questioned its claim on American loyalty.

It was the simplest of games. It was the most intricately beautiful. It was unencumbered by the gimmicks, gadgets and puffery that surrounds today's version. None of the extraneous decorations were necessary. We had baseball. What else could anyone possibly need?

Baseball held a special grip on almost every Detroiter's heart. It was a game for the average working person. And what American city was more working class than Detroit?

Detroit was not New York with its panoply of investment and advertising and publishing firms. It wasn't Boston with its blend of modern business and old world charm. It wasn't Chicago with its own brand of working class and the Midwest's answer to New York.

It was Detroit—a basically blue-collar city that centered around the auto industry. Back then—and today—people are tough in Detroit. But the toughness is borne out of an unflappable work ethic. As hard as Detroit's exterior appears to be, it is inversely as warm on the inside.

Perhaps more than in most major cities, Detroiters demonstrate a tendency to remain in the metropolitan area after reaching adulthood. Consequently, traditions pass from one generation to the next.

Few loyalties are as strong as those shared by Detroiters. It's the nature of their make-up. It's the inherent beauty of a proud working class.

It's critical to understand the nature of the city into which John Earl Fetzer entered the game of baseball. Without an appreciation for what Detroit was and how it had evolved, it's impossible to reach a meaningful interpretation of the man.

I was just a kid in 1956 when Fetzer came into the game. It was during that magical time known as "baseball's golden era." I didn't care much about who owned the Tigers back then. Not as long as Al Kaline and Harvey Kuenn and Jim Bunning and Frank Lary and the rest of the Tigers were playing.

I was lucky to see all of those players during the most delightful period of baseball history. Then I really hit the jackpot. Far beyond my wildest dreams. After all, how could any kid from the neighborhood dare to dream he'd grow up to cover the Tigers as baseball beat writer for one of the Detroit daily newspapers and then later work for the team?

As unlikely as that unfolding, how could anyone realize that with Fetzer's arrival, baseball unknowingly became the recipient of a true renaissance man?

Already one of the nation's most financially successful entrepreneurs, Fetzer didn't need baseball to build a financial fortune. He was a particularly private person and certainly didn't need the celebrity that accompanies baseball ownership.

Fetzer brought a vision to baseball that extended far above all the mundane boundaries of business. That vision helped to shape the course of baseball history far beyond his three-decade stay.

As with most visionaries who are ahead of their times, Fetzer was a collection of intriguing contradictions. Wealthy beyond even his wildest imaginings, he placed baseball on a pedestal where success was not something to be measured by any amount of money.

Although traditional in his values and conservative by all outward appearances, Fetzer was a revolutionary in his exploration of the boldly imaginative concept of unifying body, mind and spirit into an energy whole.

Although he never demanded the distinction, he was almost always referred to as "Mr. Fetzer." It mattered little who was speaking, it just seemed the right thing to do.

His reverence for the American work ethic was reflected in his respect for the city which was acknowledged to be the working man's capitol of the United States. It was for that reason he kept the Tigers in Detroit.

His passion for baseball was reflected in his nearly three-decade leadership in the game as one of the sport's most influential figures. It was for that reason the game survived some of its most volatile economic times. Above all else, Fetzer embraced a romantic appreciation for the game. For him, baseball symbolized our national essence.

Fetzer tirelessly struggled to unify owners from both the American and National Leagues for the long range good of the game. His most celebrated success was a unified national television contract which pioneered the way for today's almost unthinkable riches.

Fetzer believed in the traditional spirit of baseball. It served as the conscience of America. The game did not belong to the owners or players. It was to be shared equally by every man, woman, boy and girl. Baseball was a gift to be treasured, not an instrument of gimmicks to be used solely for profit.

Fetzer believed that baseball belonged to the average working man. It was a game for the family. The price of a ticket should remain within the factory worker's reach. The game was never intended to serve as a mere corporate marketing tool.

In almost every slice of American history, there comes a time when certain pieces from the past just don't seem to fit with the present. For whatever reason, whether it be external force or something created from within, a metamorphosis occurs. Power brokers of the moment call such change progress. Progress, of course, is always subjective.

Some changes are quickly embraced by the majority. Others are accepted only when tempered by time. Ford's Thunderbird, for instance, is a handsome, mid-size vehicle. Those who remember the two-seater original, however, may never fully reconcile today's version with the way it used to be.

Change is at least mildly challenged regardless of its apparent inevitability. Most often, change is good because it addresses the issues of the present. Usually the passing of time gently heals any divisive wounds.

It's dangerous, though, for makers of change to tinker with the American conscience. Matters touched by tradition and spirit are reconciled slowly, if ever at all.

And so it is with baseball. Because, justifiably or not, for most of a century the game enjoyed a position of reverence as America's Pastime. As with politics, education, medicine, the law, and at times religion, however, even the great game is not immune from inevitable change.

Sometimes change is real, involving the actual mutation of rules and elements surrounding the sport. Other times change is merely perceptual. What once was considered as the standard by which excellence is measured, no longer is accepted.

Whether change is actually real is a matter to be judged solely by the perceiver. But doesn't one's perception make it real for those who believe?

American novelist John Steinbeck succinctly addresses this phenomenon of perception when he analyzes a changing America in his classic work, *Travels with Charley*:

"It would be pleasant to be able to say of my travels with Charley, 'I went out to find the truth about my country and I found it.' And then it would be such a simple matter to set down my findings and lean back comfortably with a fine sense of having discovered truths and taught them to my readers. I wish it were that easy. But what I carried in my head and deeper in my perceptions was a barrel of worms. I discovered long ago in collecting and classifying marine animals that what I found was closely intermeshed with how I felt at the moment. External reality has a way of being not so external after all.

"This monster of a land, this mightiest of nations, this spawn of the future, turns out to be the macrocosm of microcosm me. If an Englishman or a Frenchman or an Italian should travel my route, see what I saw, hear what I heard, their stored pictures would be not only different from mine but equally different from one another. If other Americans reading this account should feel it true, that agreement would only mean that we are alike in our Americanness."

The same principle applies to baseball. Perception is measured by the moment. While the traditionalist remains steadfast that the game will never be as whole as in the "good old days," is it not merely a matter of perception impossible to measure by empirical standards?

The contemporary fan seems to have accepted the glut of labor relations problems and marketing gimmickry as part of the game. That simplicity of spirit that once separated baseball from the rest of big business no longer exists.

Baseball once was a sport in which major deals were done on a handshake. Now it takes teams of lawyers to come to the same decision. And then it requires an army of marketing salesmen to convince the public that the decision was the right one for the good of the game.

Was it better in the past when the game was "the thing"? That was a time when baseball's essence was almost spiritual with no need for modern marketing madness.

Or has today's hybrid begun to create a history of its own? Have fans come to accept multi-million dollar standoffs between owners and players which, for the most part, have been fueled by the sins of corporate America?

The answer, of course, lies simply in perception.

One thing for certain is that passion for baseball once universally shared even by fans who did not frequent games has been replaced. It's been replaced by greater numbers at the parks and a far greater gross income for the sport and its participants than ever once was imaginable.

A national love affair bordering upon patriotism has been tempered by unheard of riches to soothe the pain of separation. And is not that reflective of modern corporate America?

Despite anyone's preference, baseball has definitely changed. To this, both traditionalist and corporate advocate have no recourse but to agree. Is the game better or worse for it? Perhaps there's no single suitable answer. The question is best answered solely by perception.

Fetzer was a proponent of change. He wrestled with his peers to make baseball more contemporary. From reducing the number of games on the schedule to an additional round of playoffs to the concept of inter-league play, Fetzer was a pioneer. Never, however, did he dare tamper with the essence of the game. That was sacred, something no owner should touch.

Fetzer was the last in the line of sportsmen/owners. They were successful businessmen in their own right. But they were careful to separate their business interests from baseball. They were vigilant never to allow the game to be transformed into a vehicle of corporate consumerism.

Whether baseball is better or worse today is a judgment call based upon individual perception. The fact that baseball is different from the time when Fetzer presided as one of the powers behind the throne, however, is undeniable.

I simply remember all the good times when baseball stood above comparison to all other sports. I remember its purity and ability to enchant a nation simply by its innocence on major league diamonds and dusty sandlots all across the country.

For these memories I thank all of baseball's players, managers, executives and owners who perpetuated a belief that transcended the game on the field.

I particularly thank John Earl Fetzer. He kept alive my conviction in the game. He provided Tiger fans everywhere magical memories that never will be erased.

I was very fortunate to have written about and worked in the game I so loved. The memories are beautiful. None are quite as warm as those wonderful walks down Michigan Avenue.

CHAPTER 1

There Was a Time

There was a time, and not so long ago, when America's love affair with baseball was as much a given as turkey dinner on Thanksgiving. Not by just the diehards who could recite even the most obscure batting or pitching record like some unforgettable nursery rhyme. But by every man and woman who ever swung a bat on a sandlot in their youth.

This loyalty to the game was openly displayed, like the American flag on the Fourth of July. The game transcended all the balls, strikes and volumes of statistics swallowed by all the figure filberts like handfuls of Crackerjack.

Baseball, by its nature, is comprised of an endless stream of numbers. They are part of its charm. Part of the romance that strings years and decades together into what we have come to appreciate as tradition.

The spirit of the game, however, lifted baseball to a level that all these numbers couldn't reach. That spirit was a symbol of trust and tradition. National crises fill our history books. The problems of daily life indiscriminately pepper everyone from doctor to lawyer to plumber.

Regardless of all uncertainties, however, baseball always stayed a step above all of life's banalities. It was hardly a cure for any malady, large or small; but like a trusted friend, it always was there.

Even if misplaced, baseball was accorded the position of serving as a national conscience. There were winners. There were losers. But all games were played with dignity. Honesty and integrity were the cornerstones of baseball's foundation. There were simple rules that everyone knew. Often the measure of success was not determined simply by victory or defeat. Baseball belonged to everyone. And the game was more reliable than a sellout on Opening Day. It was always there for everyone's taking.

With a collection of historical heroes, coupled with all its subtle pastoral charm, baseball cast a spell over the nation. It was impossible to escape. Not everyone embraced the sport. But hardly any could ignore it. Since its inception at the start of the century, baseball had come to be accepted as America's game.

Baseball believers spanned the spectrum of our society. Businessmen to blue-collar workers. Career women to housewives. Retirees to grade schoolers. There were favorite teams. Favorite players. Favorite memories. Some followers may have been passive. But detractors flirted with treason.

Some fans studied the game like a science. Others, at least, remained familiar with the hometown team's score.

Regardless of the intensity of its followers, baseball enjoyed a niche of near royal reverence. To some it was a religion. From all, it commanded respect.

Other professional sports boasted their own armies of believers. Before the National Football League established itself as a Sunday afternoon television staple, there was a hard-core collection of football fanatics. Before the marketing miracle of the National Basketball Association, the sport was supported by its own cult of junkies. In the six original cities of the National Hockey Association, there was a somewhat restricted fervor. But even today after layers of expansion, the NHL is still trying to become a sport for American masses.

Despite the growing popularity of these other sports, there was a time when all were played merely to fill the gap between the World Series and spring training.

If not infectiously, baseball, at least passively, captured the imagination of all America for most of a century. Springs and summers were measured by various points of the season—Opening Day, the All-Star Game, the dog days of August, the September salary drives and pennant pushes. Winters were gauged by the number of days remaining until spring training—that wonderful time of year that reminds us that the sun, flowers and green grass truly are on their way back to a frozen north.

The game produced figures by whom standards of excellence were measured. Writers have romanticized baseball's pastoral charm. Historians have documented each pitch of its unfolding chronology. Analysts have dissected the simplest statistic to the point of being able to judge the talents of a player without ever actually having seen him perform.

No other sport has so colorfully invaded our everyday language with its jargon as has baseball. "You're in the ballpark," or "You struck out on that deal," for instance, are phrases used freely, even by Americans who have never visited a stadium.

There was a time when personal lifelong memories were created from visits to the park. Father to son to next generation rituals were conceived through the evolution of the game. Role models have been made of the performers who play a little boys' game for big-time money.

Except for a few minor adjustments, the rules of the game still remain pretty much the same as from the turn of the century. Nine innings to a game. Four balls a walk. Three strikes and out. Ninety feet to each base. Sixty feet, six inches from the mound to the plate. Over the fence a home run. And no time limit, regardless of the score.

The stability of the game lies at the core of its beauty. In a society that evolved primarily from farming to industrial to high tech, the reliability of baseball remained a comforting constant throughout a sometimes volatile transformation.

During the last dozen years, however, baseball's internal workings have undergone radical mutation. The baseball purist may suggest "mutilated" as a more appropriate term. Regardless of interpretation, the game has been imprinted with significant change.

Once a game of the workingman and his family, baseball now has been transformed into a modern corporate tool. Commercialization has replaced the simplicity of a Sunday afternoon at the ballpark. Much of the game's pastoral tranquillity has been swallowed by insatiable marketing hype. Baseball now is peddled to the public like a used car or some revolutionary hybrid silk stocking. And the game is sold in pieces to anyone with enough dollars to meet some outrageous price tag. From autographs to pictures to replica jerseys to the very names of the parks, nothing remains sacred and detached from the commercial blanket of profit. Everything has its price.

There was that time, though, when baseball transcended all the banalities of contemporary corporate life. The terms "lawsuit" and "pennant race" were a blasphemous mix. Deals were done on handshakes. The power of a man's word superseded any dozen-page legal contract. For their summers, players earned better than a workingman's wage. They filled off-seasons with jobs in the everyday world.

And, yes, that was a time when autographs weren't sold for profit. Names of the ballparks were restricted to time-honored traditions. "Luxury boxes" didn't have sofas, swivel chairs, wet bars or hors d'ouvres. They were a half dozen prime seats close to the hot dog stand in the bleachers. And the game on the field—not a fireworks display or laser show—was the feature attraction for a visit to the park.

For those too young to appreciate such times, it demands a suspension of belief. For those blessed by maturity that permits such recollection, it may require a mental nudge to recall times so simply spent.

Detroit, at that time, was a sportsman's paradise. While waiting for the baseball season, fans filled their falls rooting for the Lions to repeat the glory years of Bobby Layne. Winters were spent marveling at the legend of the Red Wings' Gordie Howe. The Pistons, with Hall of Famer George Yardley, had yet to make their move from Fort Wayne, Indiana to Detroit.

The year was tightly packed. There was plenty to satisfy the appetite of even the most ravenous sportsman. But it was the Tigers around which the year was planned.

The Tigers, of course, long had been one of the most storied franchises in professional sports. The tradition was born in 1901 when they became a charter member of the American League. The game's working-class flavor quickly found a comfortable home in a workingman's town.

Since before the turn of the century, Detroit had been primarily a blue-collar town. The explosion of the auto industry expanded those roots. The marriage of blue-collar workers and baseball was a perfect match. It was as natural as a doubleheader on a sunny Sunday in June.

Detroiters and baseball made for a beautiful romantic coupling. And the games played at the corner of Michigan and Trumbull were only part of the bond.

Amateur baseball thrived on city sandlots. Detroit's dusty diamonds became the springboards of countless big league dreams. From Northwestern Field on the West Side to Manz Field on the East, Detroit was a festival of first-rate sandlot action. Spectators filled the wooden bleachers. Along with New York and St. Louis, Detroit was a fertile feeding ground for professional leagues at every level.

Kids not playing on the sandlots set up makeshift diamonds in alleys and on the streets. Sometimes home plate was a mere crack in the concrete of a paved alley. A parked auto's right taillight often served as first base when the game moved to the street. Cracked bats were nailed and tightly taped. Worn baseballs were wrapped in black friction tape. Kids took turns at pretending they were their favorite players. Al Kaline was the most popular choice. Harvey Kuenn was good, but always finished as runner-up. Young pitchers pictured themselves as Jim Bunning or Frank Lary. No matter where the game was played, there was a daily dose of baseball. Every kid in the neighborhood got his fair share of swings.

The Tigers, of course, occupied a sacred position of community prominence. Regardless where they finished in the standings, the Tigers always stood as the darlings of Detroit.

A trip to Briggs Stadium, now Tiger Stadium, was a treasured summer outing. It became a family tradition. Fathers, mothers, sons and daughters planned each excursion weeks ahead.

For families without an automobile, transportation was never a problem. Electric-powered streetcars and city buses stopped right at the corner of Michigan and Trumbull. Ticket prices were within the reach of every auto worker. Night games were fewer. Sunday doubleheaders were a special treat.

Player trades have always tickled the imaginations of the fans. But local heroes often spent whole careers in one town. Heroes like those became part of everyone's family. Kids memorized all the player statistics quicker than their multiplication tables in school.

There were problems in those days, for sure. Looking back, however, those problems seemed part of a much simpler time. And part of the very essence of that peaceful beauty was the quiet reassurance of baseball; a common, unifying thread. Now that time seems to be almost make-believe. Was it really all so simple?

Those days truly did exist. Ironically, that nostalgia is exactly what today's marketing strategists try so desperately to re-create. With a bag of hard-sell gimmicks that seem to be drawn from a bottomless pit, they attempt to create the illusion of baseball's idyllic past.

Despite all their resources and methods of masquerade, attempts to manufacture that feeling are hollow. It's ironic that contemporary corporate America led to the suffocation of the spirit it is now trying to imitate. America's affair with baseball was born of love not created by an advertising campaign.

Along with a "golden age" of players, it was an equally glorious time of revered baseball franchise owners. They were more than mere holders of the deeds. They were the guardians of the game. They were entrusted with the protection of a national treasure. They had to do the right thing.

It was an era of splendid sportsmen. These were the owners who had amassed fortunes in an assortment of business ventures. Some were industrialists. Others were holders of long-time family fortunes. They all shared a common bond. They carefully segregated their business operations from their ballclubs and ran their franchises more for sport than lopsided plusses on a corporate ledger sheet.

Their time has certainly passed. They've been replaced, for the most part, by faceless corporations whose leaders all dress in pin-striped suits. The legend of these sportsmen, however, remains alive today. Dan Topping of the Yankees. Walter O'Malley of the Dodgers. Horace Stoneham of the Giants. Tom Yawkey of the Red Sox. Calvin Griffith of the Senators. John Galbreath of the Pirates. Phil Wrigley of the Cubs. And Walter O. Briggs of the Tigers.

They were the dream makers. They put all the pieces together. From the field to the fans, memories took shape. Before becoming memories, trips to the ballpark were savored. And they were passed from one generation to the next.

Operating a ball club in those days carried extraordinary responsibilities. Like the bosses at General Motors or Ford, owners competed for a part of their loyalists' dollar. But they also were charged with the safekeeping of their fans' forgiving hearts.

There was an unwritten code of honor among the baseball bosses. Lawyers had their place; but not on the front office staff of a major league baseball club.

Owners pledged their allegiance to an almost sacred commitment. Not only to the community in which a club played, but also to the game. Violation of those unwritten responsibilities was simply not acceptable. No one was big enough to tinker with

Mother's Day. Or the Thanksgiving Day Christmas Parade. And certainly not baseball.

Especially not the Tigers in Detroit!

John E. Fetzer didn't charge into this golden age of baseball with the fanfare that sometimes accompanies modern entries. Along with ten partners, he tip-toed carefully and quietly. His characteristic reticence was complemented by a design and vision for which only history is equipped to judge.

John Fetzer was indeed anonymous. But he was destined to leave an indelible imprint that remains today.

Through the shaping of a national television contract by which all teams share revenues equally, Fetzer paved the way for the billion-dollar industry into which the game has evolved. He struggled for a unity of spirit and action among owners of both leagues. After serving on baseball's highest councils and committees, he unceremoniously walked away when the sores of corporate manipulations began to disfigure the innocence of a boys' game.

It was the game that had helped to paint the history of America. As passionate for baseball as he remained throughout his life, Fetzer kissed his love good-bye when the last of its innocence seemed to be squeezed by the quest for corporate profit.

Fetzer was first a remarkably disciplined and blatantly successful businessman. He amassed a fortune as a pioneer in the broadcast industry. Starting virtually with nothing, he created an empire consisting of radio and television station holdings that stretched across the country.

He was shrewd, tireless and imaginative. He also was straightforward and honest. He shared a genuine concern for baseball and its measure of a nation. For that, he commands a place of prominence among his peers and the revered owners who preceded him.

Unlike some of those peers, however, Fetzer was a visionary. He was consumed with extending the boundaries of baseball. The game was heading straight into the face of impending economic and perhaps moral chaos. Like the social upheaval of the turbulent '60s, the resulting funnel of revolution has yet to be totally sorted out.

Fetzer's vision of the future served as a life rope between the turmoil of the times and the tradition of the game. Coupling good business sense with his love for the Tigers, he kept the franchise solvent and at the forefront of all professional sports.

When he left, the era of the sportsman/owner came to a quiet close. There were no more pioneering giants. The game, indeed, had passed to corporate America.

Before leaving, however, Fetzer may have preserved enough of the sport to keep it alive during its quest for its proper position of prominence in the modern era of corporate commercialism. At least his vision of baseball's existence as a unified entity is still a concept that is being struggled for today.

And if it were not for the groundwork laid by the undying spirit of John Fetzer, perhaps baseball might not be poised to rally toward the position of dominance it once enjoyed without even breaking a sweat.

There really was a time when baseball was a game for all people. It was men like Fetzer who kept the sport so simply uncluttered. It may have been Fetzer alone, among the owners, who truly understood how much that spirit meant to the nation.

CHAPTER 2

Body, Mind and Spirit

History will remember John Fetzer according to all the conventional yardsticks of success.

He was a broadcast pioneer who helped to shape the industry that defines our contemporary society. He not only owned one of professional sports' most storied franchises for more than a quarter of a century, he created a network television package that provides a billion-dollar base from which major league baseball survives today.

From the fruits of these and a variety of other business ventures, he died as one of America's wealthiest individuals. By all generally accepted standards, John Fetzer was the portrait of the American dream.

Almost anonymously, Fetzer accepted the accolades and fortune that accompany the magnitude of his business success. He appreciated his immense financial fortune, yet he lived modestly with his wife, Rhea, in a rather nondescript colonial home in Kalamazoo, Michigan. He shyly shunned the trappings of his wealth. His sphere of influence was national. Yet he remained meticulously judicious with the power entrusted to him.

Fetzer was certainly cognizant of the rewards derived from a self-made empire in the highly visible worlds of broadcasting and baseball. They were not, however, the driving force that consumed him daily from his childhood in Indiana until his death in 1991. They served as viable tools in his search for the secret of the untapped power derived from the unity of mankind's body, mind and spirit.

It was the inherent essence of baseball—all that was good in life, in fact—that symbolized the very spirit that Fetzer pursued for a lifetime.

Fetzer, of course, accepted the conventional rewards of fortune and fame. But it was his itinerary to the unknown that generated greater satisfaction than all usual measures of enrichment. Without first accepting the significance of this unconventional yardstick, it is impossible to appreciate the scope of this truly singular man.

The concept of harmony between body, mind and spirit remains an unsolved mystery of energy mastery even today. While many discount its merit, or even its existence, scientists and philosophers grapple with its complexities. Ever so slowly, it is creeping more into the mainstream of scientific phenomenon.

Although largely unknown and certainly controversial, that spirit of unity predicated Fetzer's purpose for serving his myriad roles. Through the unity of all three elements, Fetzer believed that one day man might lift himself to a higher level of existence.

Fetzer's devotion to this unconventional approach toward life, at first glance, appears to contradict his widely held traditional public image. He was a businessman who enjoyed world-wide respect within the mainstream business community. He was fabulously wealthy, but dressed conservatively and conducted himself with the professional decorum expected of his station. His penchant for reticence created a cloak of mystery that masked his simplicity of spirit.

Yet his obsession to unlock the secrets of body, mind and spiritual unity drove Fetzer to a self-styled life of discipline and imagination. He pursued that obsession to his very last breath.

"We don't have to take a vow of poverty to be spiritual . . . . And we find fellow travelers in all areas of human endeavors," said Edgar Mitchell, who called Fetzer a "fellow traveler." Mitchell was a United States astronaut who traveled to the moon. When the NASA-trained engineer first set foot on the surface of the moon and looked at the earth, he said he felt as if something overcame him. He said he became immersed in "the universal consciousness" and was "overwhelmed with the meaning of life and the sacredness of existence."

Mitchell later founded the Institute for Noetic Sciences (from *noos,* the Greek word for mind), dedicated to the exploration of "inner space." He invited Fetzer to serve on the board of directors.

There is nothing mystical nor religious about Fetzer's belief in holistic unity. It is, instead, daring and imaginative. It was the challenge for which Fetzer took the lead throughout his private life. His public affairs generated a sufficient fortune so that he could pursue his bold venture into this mind-expanding phenomenon.

Fetzer believed that the key to humanity's future lay in the productive linkage of mind, body and spirit and the application of this holistic approach to the problems plaguing our planet. Throughout his life, Fetzer pursued answers to the mystery of man's true purpose on earth. He was determined to discover how harnessing various forms of energy might unlock the secrets to a more fulfilling world.

"I don't believe that man comes into this life to have a shallow experience, make some improvements and developments, only to fade away to nothing," Fetzer said.

At first glance, it appears romantically noble. It was, nevertheless, true that Fetzer devoted his life toward the discovery of who we are and how we might improve our existence.

"John was a very moral man," said long-time friend and former Baseball Commissioner Bowie Kuhn. "He had a certain private morality and theology very much his own. He was never an evangelist for any particular dogma. He simply was a very moral man.

"By taking the type of stance as he did, in baseball, he and I were kind of walking side by side. He was pushing a kind of morality, but in his own gentle way."

Fetzer's beliefs were ecumenical. They never embraced a particular creed. He cared not whether a person's leanings were Catholic, Protestant, Judaic, Buddhist, Hindu or any other religious dogma. He was acquainted with all religious disciplines. He cared only about the inherent morality of man. Fetzer believed that the communion of body, mind and spirit transcends each individual dogma and allows all to elevate themselves to that higher plain of excellence.

"I have always been a seeker," Fetzer said. "I have always sought the answers in those fields of inquiry that are challenging. I guess that's why I have examined things and subjects all over the world.

"Do you know what I discovered? There is a commonality, that when you lift up the epidermis and look underneath, you find

a common bond among all of the perspectives and spiritual out-
looks in the world. And that's love. Love cuts through all the differ-
ences that exist in philosophy and dogma.

"During my life, I've known many people who were successful primarily because they showed loving concern for others. They
lived the qualities of love without ever talking about it. They acted
in a loving manner and changed their little corner of the world by
doing so. Thus, I think that love is the core energy that rules everything. It is the force field out of the electronic energy of creation.
Love is the one ingredient that holds us all together.

"Loving concern is the one ingredient that can make us successful. It's the glue that binds us together. We must have dedicated
people all over the world who are willing to search, to research, to
contribute, and to become one through love. If love isn't there, our
efforts will fail. I feel my most important mission is to carry love to
this process, to nurture it and have some of it rub off on others. We
simply must have love as an institution."

Fetzer was convinced of the power of intellectual energy.
When the Tigers were in the middle of a 19-game losing streak
during the 1975 season, he made a rare clubhouse appearance to
address his team.

"I believe that each of us has the capacity to be whatever we
want to be," he said. "All outer conditions of life are related to the
inner state of mind. We are what we think we are.

"If we relate properly, our great inner potential will take care
of problems. The sky is the limit if we cultivate a belief in ourselves.
When a man suffers, he simply has to find his inner self by pictur-
ing himself on successful terms. You can't fight adversity without
looking for its cause. More often, the cause is a state of mind. Self-
control and self-discipline correct weaknesses. If you are negative
all the time, you will be a loser. If you have a positive nature, you
can be a winner."

Fetzer's holistic beliefs and wonder for unexplored sources
of energy were demonstrated early in his life by his fascination for
wireless communication. He was enamored by the electrical phenomenon early in his boyhood.

His interest blossomed and started to mature at Purdue University, which was the beginning of his collegiate career. Fetzer
was fascinated and influenced by the studies of Nikola Tesla, a Yu-
goslavian-born electrical engineer and former employee of inventor genius Thomas Edison. Tesla was a renowned experimental re-

searcher and inventor, specializing in the field of electro-magnetic energy. He experimented with the high frequency coil for the transmission of radio and radar waves. He also believed that the earth itself was a giant generator, creating in its rotation an electro-magnetic field that could power all the energy needs of mankind if it could be properly harnessed.

Fetzer was fascinated by Tesla, his theories and methodology. He marveled that electrical energy could be transformed into sound energy with no visible connectors. And this fascination led to daring speculations of his own.

Fetzer extended Tesla's theory and concluded that thought is, indeed, a form of energy. The mind is a form of energy at work. Therefore, why could there not be a somewhat wireless connector of mind to body to spirit through the energy of thought?

"Broadcasting is the underpinning of what we know and think we know," Fetzer explained. "It deals totally with energy. Experimentation in broadcasting served as the catalyst for enlarging our definition of the term energy, its applications and its force in the universal scheme of things.

"I believe the time is coming when energies of all kinds will be available, not only for diagnosing man's medical maladies. New forms and new means of transmission will come to the forefront in the future. Tesla transmitted power over the air to a point 30 miles away, where it ran motors and illuminated lights without any interconnecting wires. I think the universe is teeming with all kinds of energies that are just waiting to be discovered and to be used in personal and global healing."

Because of his reticence and his dedication to discovery, Fetzer rarely spoke publicly about his beliefs. However, many are detailed in *America's Agony,* a book he wrote and published in 1971 through the foundation he created. In it, Fetzer described the cosmos of outer space as the source of life and the whirling center of a divine intelligence. The physical man is an electronic device made up of transistor-like cells, all vibrating with cosmic energy. Learning to bridge that gap through the unification of body, mind and spiritual energy was Fetzer's noble passion.

Bruce Fetzer, one of Fetzer's few living relatives, became close to his grand-uncle and actually worked for him the last ten years of Fetzer's life. During regular weekly visits for more than a decade, Bruce recalls how his uncle not only marveled at mankind's untapped inner source of mental power, but also demonstrated some of its wonder.

"He was not a psychic," the younger Fetzer explained. "He did, however, possess an intuition—a sort of inspired intuition. It was as if he had perfected the ability to know what you were going to say even before it was spoken. John was incredibly intelligent. And yet his mental power seemed to take one step beyond the normal limits of any accepted measure of intelligence. He believed it was this type of energy that mankind has the ability to explore and capture."

Early in his career, Fetzer funded a variety of programs and projects at universities and institutes around the world to investigate this imaginative phenomenon. He later created the Fetzer Institute, to which he bequeathed his fortune, to further study this daring field that one day may unlock secrets that have lived latently within mankind for centuries.

To the uninitiated, this bold approach to body, mind and spirit, may initially appear as bizarre as wireless communication once was perceived to be. But Fetzer's passion for this yet unraveling universe of knowledge was real. And now more conventional arms of science are finally paying more attention to what once was considered pure, imaginative fancy.

Even as it gains more legitimacy, however, what does this philosophy of thought have to do with Fetzer's baseball interest? At first glance, perhaps nothing. A closer examination, however, reveals that it lies at the root of Fetzer's passion for the sport.

The financial fruits of a successful career as a broadcasting pioneer represented the combined labor of body and mind. Baseball, to Fetzer, symbolized spirit. He felt baseball represented all that was good in mankind; it served as the conscience of a country. Although baseball had to be carefully integrated with the necessary matters of the business world, it was to stand above everything mundane.

Baseball, to Fetzer, was the unchallenged measure of morality. Although it must function in a business world, the game had to keep itself at a level above the usual trappings of a society that measures success in dollars and cents.

Those in positions of leadership within the game were charged with protecting that integrity. Nothing less was acceptable. Everything more was to be pursued.

It was this sense of purpose that governed Fetzer throughout his professional career and his more than quarter-century in major league baseball.

It was this unity of body, mind and spirit that he gently tried to instill into the game that has meant so much to a nation.

CHAPTER 3

A Fork in the Road

Baseball reached its crossroads toward the end of the 1983 season. There's no asterisk in the record books. No one can pinpoint the precise moment of definition.

It was like when evening drifts gently into night. Evening stops. Night arrives. Silently, darkness surrounds everything without a precise beginning.

Baseball's shift in direction was equally subtle. At least at the start. Soon it became evident the game had conclusively reached a fork in the road of its history.

Baseball made a decision. It was this decision that prompted the beginning of the end of John Fetzer's baseball career. And it is that decision that best provides a perspective on Fetzer's life in baseball—beginning, middle and end.

Baseball's decision was more philosophical than moral. Yet it danced dangerously close to the core of the game's soul.

Quite subtly at first and now blatantly obvious, major league baseball chose the path of commercialism over the tradition-rich road it had traveled since the turn of the century. Hardly a sin, yet it remains a distasteful departure, particularly for purists who share a near religious zeal for the game.

"John Fetzer was a living symbol of everything baseball represented," said Bowie Kuhn, who served as the game's Commissioner from 1969 through 1984. "There's no question he could never have tolerated the path which baseball ultimately chose."

The tradition of baseball's high moral ground dates back to 1921 when the game invited Judge Kenesaw Mountain Landis to join as its first Commissioner. Baseball's very integrity had been rocked by the Black Sox scandal of 1919. The game, often referred to as the national conscience, had been blindsided. It was forced to kneel in shame.

Landis was commissioned to cleanse all impurities. His charge was to lift this proud institution to a level above every normal measure of morality.

"There was a kind of reformation that hit baseball after the Black Sox scandal," Kuhn explained. "That reformation drove baseball to a very high ground.

"Landis would preach about baseball's moral obligations and how we in the game had to serve as good examples. We should be self-regulated and government de-regulated. Our integrity should be at such a high level that we would be capable of regulating ourselves. John had great respect for that concept.

"That very concept and John Fetzer were a couple of primary reasons I took the job as Commissioner. It wasn't for financial reasons. I could have done much better financially through the practice of law."

Certainly, baseball's decision to choose the path of corporate commercialism did not violate any moral standards. As a matter of fact, it put baseball hand-in-hand with contemporary corporate America.

But it definitely tarnished the purity of the game's spirit. Mixing the banalities of big business with the simplicity of baseball's being is like turning a family picnic into a carnival—complete with midway, barkers and shill games. Fetzer wanted no part of a traveling medicine show.

"John had such a great respect for the institution of baseball," Kuhn said. "He truthfully cared about the game. He was a very moral man.

"He applied that morality to the concept of baseball. He pushed a consistent message of morality. There was a strong, old-fashioned almost puritan morality in John. He was always pushing the message of 'We just can't do the wrong thing. It's not permissible. We can't cheat or lie or do improper things. We have to do the right thing. We're baseball.'"

By 1983, either by attrition or simple frustration from the direction baseball was headed, almost all the sportsmen/owners had left the game. They were replaced by a new breed who brought with them a revolutionary philosophy of operation. They were the fronts for faceless corporations. They were the standard bearers of the commercialism that riddles the sport today.

"There's no question baseball made that decision somewhere back in the early to mid '80s," Kuhn concurred.

And with that decision, Fetzer believed the game he had so dearly cherished was soon to travel a path that ran counter to the spirit that baseball had so proudly espoused.

Fetzer was not the come-to-life embodiment of Ray Kinsella from the popular movie, *Field of Dreams.* He was, however, a dreamer himself who chose not to compromise his personal standards.

Certainly Fetzer wasn't unique in his near-religious regard for the spiritual good he felt the game generated. Baseball purists date back to the turn of the century. Fetzer realized, however, that he was in a position to protect the sanctity of the game. And he defended that charge until there were no more sportsmen/owners left to rally to the challenge.

Fetzer became concerned about his sport years before he decided to leave.

"Baseball had an awful lot going for it to withstand all of the crap coming its way," he said. "What worried the devil out of me was the fact that the big-business syndrome had invaded our sport. That, of course, attracted big labor. The family-owned franchise was becoming a dinosaur. Big corporations were buying the teams and running them like a division. That was taking some of the romance out of the game for me."

French author Jacques Barzun wrote: *"Whoever wants to know the heart and mind of America had better learn baseball."* This worthy insight might be rearranged to suggest that whoever wants to know the heart and mind of John Fetzer had better learn his appreciation for the game.

Fetzer's feel for baseball transcended all of its financial attachments in the same manner as the game transcended all the scores, statistics and numbers.

It was more than a game for America. For Fetzer, it served as a microcosm for every dream of every American, whether he had been blessed by financial fortune or worked the assembly line in one of Detroit's auto plants.

In its own peculiar way, baseball made sense out of an all-too-chaotic world. Baseball offered a sense of propriety. There was order. And there were specific rules—some written and some unwritten—that had to be followed. There were winners. There were losers. Winners were not necessarily the swiftest. Most of the time, however, victory went to those who persevered through adversity.

Baseball provided purpose. It colored our history. For winners and losers alike, always there was hope. Baseball was the most forgiving of sports. A second chance was only one day away. As long as the game was played according to all the established traditional rules, baseball served as a measure of American initiative. Indeed, it had become symbolic of a national spirit.

"Baseball is much more than the measure of which team can score more runs than another," Fetzer said. "It is the one game by which we are able to gauge the good in our society.

"Baseball not only reflected American life, it left an indelible mark upon it. It contributed color and flavor to our language, provided a theme for song, story, and stage, and supplied many names to the galaxy of American folk heroes.

"In short, baseball was ballet without music, drama without words, carnival without kewpie dolls, circus without clowns. It was as simple as a ball and bat, yet as complex as the American spirit it symbolized—a sport, a business, and sometimes even a religion."

Because of his enormous wealth and national stature, there's a tendency to view Fetzer as a complicated man. The National League embracing the designated hitter rule is closer to the truth. He was, without doubt, a man of many contradictions. But he was a simple man who believed in simple truths. Hard work. Organization. Respect for human dignity. And he believed strongly that baseball was the one American gift that encompassed all of these elements.

Fetzer possessed an enormous simplicity of spirit. It was accompanied, however, by an equally enormous set of contradictions. He was a reticent man who was a pioneer in the untapped industries of radio and television. He spoke with an economy of words, but possessed the vocabulary of an Ivy League scholar. He carved a self-made fortune that made him one of America's wealthiest individuals, yet he followed the modest lifestyle of an average working man. He was the textbook portrayal of big business success, yet he ferociously guarded baseball against being swallowed by corporate excess.

Former Tiger Manager Jack Tighe offered one of the most subtle, yet perhaps most insightful, reflections on the character of Fetzer. Tighe first joined the Tiger organization as a player in 1935. He got his first minor-league managing job at Muskegon, Michigan in 1940. He was Fetzer's first manager in 1957 after the syndicate officially took control of the Tigers. He was replaced as manager during the 1958 season, but continued to work for the Tigers as a special assignment scout until after Mike Ilitch purchased the team in 1992. He worked for the Tigers for 54 years.

Tighe was the prototype for the old-time baseball manager and possessed a devilish passion for life. He had gravel in his voice and laced his phrases with appropriately placed obscenities. He loved the game and spun stories like George Burns. He had a wonderful gift for being able to laugh at himself. His gruff exterior camouflaged the wisdom and sensitivity of the old-time parish priest.

Tighe's position in baseball often thrust him into the company of influential business elites. He felt more comfortable with a cigar between his fingers telling the hard hats at the corner bar why he made a pitching change in the seventh inning.

"Mr. Fetzer made a lot of money and accomplished a lot of great things," Tighe offered. "But let me tell you something that might give you a better picture of what was inside the man.

"You could sit down and talk to the man. He didn't put himself up on some pedestal and not let anyone get to him. He had a chain of command as far as business goes. But you could talk to him like you were talking to a long-time friend. And he'd listen.

"Why do you think all of his people with the Tigers and all of his TV stations stayed so loyal all their lives? That's a tremendous tribute. That's the way he was.

"Nobody ever said anything bad about him. Think about that. Here was this big-time business multi-millionaire who could do anything he wanted to do. And you never heard any scandals about him. He didn't lie. He didn't cheat. He didn't run around.

"Working for him was like working for your friend. He always managed to be your friend. He was on a different level. Everybody called him Mr. Fetzer because it just seemed like the natural thing to do. Even Jim (Campbell) did it. But he was still your friend."

Fetzer was conservative in his approach to business matters. Yet his imagination refused to be contained by convention. In baseball, for instance, he was one of the leading proponents of the designated hitter rule. He helped to shape the format of divisions within the leagues for the purpose of playoffs before the World Series. He seriously entertained the idea of limited inter-league play. He was unafraid to consider almost any revolutionary concept, as long as it did not violate the essence of baseball's spirit.

The simplicity of Fetzer's spirit dictated these contradictions in his approach toward baseball and life. One without the other would not have equaled the man. And like the beauty of a complex poem, the meaning is often masked by the simplicity of its rhyme.

Contrary to one school of thought regarding Fetzer, he did not remain in baseball to become wealthy. He already had accomplished that long before first buying into the Detroit Tigers.

For Fetzer, the game represented the highest ideal of our national conscience. He felt privileged to serve as guardian of its tradition and honor.

"Money is not an end in itself," Fetzer said. "It's been amply shown that money does not bring happiness. And money cannot be a clock of what a person is actually worth. If it is, then I think you're on the wrong track.

"Anybody that has possessions, anybody who is very honest, will say, 'I don't own anything—my possessions all own me.'

"If man were to be judged solely by the amount of money he had accumulated during a lifetime, I suppose one might label me as having been quite a success. Money, however, serves as a poor measure of a person's real value. There are so many other more significant factors than volume of dollars that serve as the true test of a person's worth." Fetzer was referring to the spiritual—not religious—side of mankind.

There was a distinct spiritual aspect to the man who would grow to become one of history's most influential figures in broadcasting and baseball. It was this spiritual bent that served as his beacon throughout his brilliant career.

First and foremost, Fetzer was a businessman. He thrived on the gratification derived from the practice of sound, innovative and ethical business principles. With his wire rimmed glasses, trim gray hair combed straight back, necktie and navy, gray or charcoal suit, Fetzer was the picture of the successful entrepreneur. With his six-foot, two-inch, well-conditioned frame, he looked like he had stepped out of a brochure for the Harvard Business School.

Fetzer was proud of his business success. He stood unashamed of the wealth it had provided him. Yet he never felt the need to flaunt it.

"Mr. Fetzer never flaunted any of his wealth or any of his possessions," said Tiger broadcaster and Hall of Famer George Kell. "He didn't have to.

"Mr. Fetzer viewed baseball in a very different way than a lot of owners. Especially today's owners. He could have made a lot more money from the club than he did. But he was more concerned that it was run properly and according to all the traditions that have gone into making the sport that it is. He felt a responsibility for taking care of the game almost as if it was a son. He had a special kind of love for the game that's hard to define."

Fetzer had a reserve that bordered on shyness. He possessed the vocabulary of a master grammarian, yet he never used it carelessly for the purpose of intimidation. He spoke softly and chose his words precisely and for a purpose. He also possessed an uncanny ability to view a situation from several perspectives.

Fetzer understood profit and loss statements. He was calculating. He was thorough. He was a mirror image of the American work ethic. He believed in hard work, long hours and a distinct plan for the future. His flamboyance was restricted to a dark checkered sport coat. He believed a whisper was heard more clearly than a shout.

His leanings were conservative. But like any successful industrial pioneer, he was disarmingly daring and always prepared to seize the moment of opportunity.

Underneath the physical appearance of "Good Gray John", as Detroit sportswriters referred to him, however, laid the imagination of a dreamer. In his own way, he was more of a rebel to society's conventional thinking than any of the political protesters that speckled American history in the revolutionary '60s.

"So many times, it would happen at meetings of owners and they all seemed to wait for John," Kuhn recalled. "You could sense it. John would be sitting back, listening for hours and often not saying a word. Talk about various aspects of critical questions would go back and forth, until it would always become obvious that they were waiting for John to speak.

"When he finally stood to address the questions, you knew that he would shape the direction of the solution to the problems. John had a brilliant mind and would outline reasons for his position carefully and dispassionately. He was almost never emotional."

It was this bubbling energy of restless inquisitiveness that drove Fetzer in all aspects of his life. Business and baseball were treated with equal respect. Both were used as vehicles in his quest to discover the power of body, mind and spiritual unity of all mankind.

Fetzer was fascinated by the relationship of an individual's personality or spirit and the body that houses those faculties. He was convinced that within each individual lies an indefinable driving force. When tapped to its potential, this force enables a person to achieve more than one thinks possible.

Long before the ten-second mark for the 100-yard dash was cracked, several sprinters possessed the physical abilities to do it. Yet it took the combined effort of body and spirit to establish a new standard. Similarly, throughout his life, Fetzer remained convinced that there exists an indefinable link between body and mind that allows humankind to achieve the seemingly unreachable. He also believed that mankind has yet to discover the answer for harnessing all of one's energies encompassing body, mind and spirit into a meaningful whole.

In 1976, a 21-year-old rookie out of the Boston area grabbed the baseball universe with the grip of a wrestler and the gentleness of a dove. He was a magnet; he transcended the game itself. He was Mark Fidrych, nicknamed "The Bird," because of his similarity to the Big Bird character of television's *Sesame Street*.

Not only was The Bird a legitimate pitching phenomenon, he was a walking, talking, come-to-life cartoon who captured the imagination of the whole country.

He wore his dirt-blond, naturally curly hair down close to the shoulders. His best jeans looked like a slice of blue limburger cheese. He believed that any shirt with a collar wasn't fit to be worn by anyone under 25. He loved kids and was always ready to sign an autograph.

On the mound he was all business. He had a vicious slider that sliced left on command, and he kept the ball wickedly low. The Bird fired strikes with the ease of flipping pennies. And to keep everything under control, he talked to the ball. Not only did the baseball listen to him that year, so did the whole nation. When The Bird talked, everybody listened.

They listened because he spoke with the innocence of a kid playing stickball on the street. It was the slang of the times. But it was laced with good, old-fashioned common sense.

Fetzer was not a collector of sports paraphernalia. However, the only autographed baseball he kept on his desk was one from

The Bird. He did this because he felt Fidrych's innocence physically reflected baseball's soul.

As the phenomenon of The Bird got hotter in that magical summer, Fetzer had General Manager Jim Campbell summon the prize of his flock to his office before a game.

"It was really something," Fidrych recalled. "I mean, Mr. Fetzer, man. He wanted to talk to me. He was the boss. He was what baseball was all about."

After Fidrych arrived from the clubhouse, Campbell left the office so Fetzer and The Bird could talk alone.

"People might think it's weird, but I remember sitting across the desk from him," Fidrych said. "He picked out some object on the desk and said, 'You know, Mark, if you concentrate hard enough on this object, you can make it move. We have that power. That's what you are actually doing to this whole city. You are making it move.'

"I didn't understand exactly what he was talking about. That stuff was heavy duty. But I knew there was something special about him. He made more sense than anybody I ever heard. He was brilliant. He had all this power. He could do anything in the world. But I never saw him abuse that power. Like I said, there was something special about him."

There may have been more similarity between Fetzer and Fidrych than anyone realizes. One thing for certain, however, was that Fetzer truly did possess "something special about him."

This quest for perfect individual harmony was the driving force behind all of Fetzer's endeavors as he carved out a financial fortune—first in the broadcast industry and later in baseball.

Baseball, without question, served as Fetzer's symbol of spiritual unity. He regarded the game as a near-religious reflection of all that's good in a yet-to-be-sorted-out cosmos.

"One of my prime purposes as owner of the Detroit Tigers was to carry forward one of the great American ideals in that good sportsmanship should become an all-consuming desire of our youth and of those oldsters who refuse to allow adult sophistication to displace the innocence of youthful fun at the ballpark," Fetzer said. "I considered the ownership of the ball club as a public trust. I was reluctantly extended the right to own the club. I never really owned the club. I served merely as its steward."

Fetzer understood that baseball was served best with the application of sound business principles. Yet he was always vigilant so as never to let big business gobble the spirit of the game which, for Fetzer, symbolized unity.

Fetzer was consumed by his drive to instill unity among his fellow owners for the long-range good of the game. He was a pioneer in demonstrating what unity of spirit could accomplish in the game. Almost single-handedly, he designed a national television contract for the game. In it, each club shared equally in the revenues. Without it, some clubs faced flat-out bankruptcy.

"I think it's fair to say that it was John Fetzer's efforts decades ago that led to the billion-dollar TV contracts that baseball enjoys today," said former American League President Lee MacPhail.

This unity of baseball ownership certainly was an extension of Fetzer's approach to life. It was a philosophy that reflected the contradictory simplicity of the man. And it was this collection of contradictions that marked John Fetzer—the conservative revolutionary—for a place in baseball history.

CHAPTER 4

Building an Empire

There was an aura surrounding John Fetzer that sometimes mistakenly marked him as being aloof.

This aura criss-crossed the lines of physical and spiritual. It gifted him with an overpowering presence wherever he appeared.

It's difficult to explain; most true leaders are blessed with it. Without even saying a word, they just appear to be in control. It's more than mere physical appearance. They radiate a sense of calm. Their confidence seems unshakable.

Fetzer possessed that presence. It's impossible to learn and not for sale at any price. If he ever became rattled, it was masterfully hidden. He was always the captain in complete control.

"I'm not smart enough to explain why," said former life-long Tiger employee and one-time manager of the Tigers, Jack Tighe. "But when Mr. Fetzer walked into a room you could just sense this aura all around him. It didn't matter who was in there with him—bankers, politicians, athletes, leaders of all kinds. When he showed up, all the other guys were relegated to secondary roles."

In 1981, celebrated CBS commentator Charles Osgood addressed major league baseball at its annual winter convention. He publicly displayed his regard for Fetzer with the following humorous anecdote.

"Mr. Fetzer and the Pope were designated to meet their Maker on the same day and were on the same elevator going up," Osgood began. "The Pope was given a little mud hut as his quarters. It was very plain, but the Pontiff was just happy to be there. Mr. Fetzer, on the other hand, was assigned a spacious, sumptuous, and luxurious room with a sensational view of the sky and with celestial Muzak playing in the background. Being a humble man, Mr. Fetzer asked the winged bellhop if there had been some mistake. He had this palatial mansion and the Pope was in the peanut gallery. No, there was no mistake. The room assignments were right. Heaven had seen a lot of Popes, but Mr. Fetzer was the first baseball owner to make the trip."

Even in his younger days, Fetzer looked as if he had been born to dress in a tastefully subtle, dark business suit. Tall in stature and always impeccably attired, he was the picture of the successful conservative businessman.

His confidence reflected an inner peace. Always polite and quick to smile, Fetzer's demeanor was complemented by an inexhaustible curiosity. He was naturally shy, but shared a genuine concern for all those he touched. Except for the physical appearance, however, there was nothing aloof about John Fetzer.

There was a peaceful reticence about Fetzer that was not the result of a crippled vocabulary. His command of the English language was as strong as Bill Gates' grip on computer technology. He had a great love for words and consequently chose each one precisely. He used each word as if it were meant for no other sentence. His mind ran overtime devising daring plans during a volatile business era in American economic history, and he easily derived more satisfaction from creating opportunities than wasting time boasting about their success.

"John was a true statesman," said former Baseball Commissioner Bowie Kuhn. "He was a man who automatically drew a lot of respect from those around him.

"He was warm-hearted without being affable. His style wasn't affability. He was warm-hearted, though, and decent. He had a great respect for the dignity of man."

Because of his rigid, modest reserve and the fact that all of his companies were privately held, no one truly knew the expanse of Fetzer's financial fortune. The magnitude of those holdings, however, easily put it into the hundreds of millions.

Fetzer's net worth placed him comfortably among baseball's most affluent franchise owners. His fortune, however, was considerably less significant than his influence on the game. Among his peers, Fetzer was universally acknowledged to be one of the most powerful forces.

In 1975 after Fetzer convinced the rest of the American League owners to approve the sale of the Chicago White Sox to the rebellious Bill Veeck, revered *Chicago Tribune* sports writer Jerome Holtzman commented on Fetzer's quiet power.

"He (Fetzer) speaks with a soft voice," Holtzman said. "But when he does speak, they (owners) listen. He's easily the most powerful man in the American League. And for the last 20 years, he has been a really dominant force in baseball—and nobody knows about it."

That's the way Fetzer designed it. For Fetzer, power was not a possession to flaunt. He believed that the real meaning of power was the ability to do something . . . coupled with the wisdom of choosing to do the right thing. Never did he abuse his power to manipulate an unfair advantage for his Detroit Tigers. On matters pertaining to baseball, Fetzer always demonstrated more concern for the long-range good of the game than he did for the immediate needs of his own team.

"Mr. Fetzer always felt that if something was good for baseball, then in the long run, it would be good for the Tigers," said long-time Tiger boss Jim Campbell. "The designated hitter rule is a good example. Mr. Fetzer and Dan Topping (owner of the Yankees) talked about it long before it came up for a vote."

The designated hitter was designed to put spark into the American League.

"Let's face it," Fetzer said, "most of the American League was not doing too well in attendance at that time. Those who were promotion-oriented felt we needed some kind of gimmick that would have an impact on our gate. The idea was to keep a name ball player on the team as a pinch-hitter deluxe, and possibly put some more runs on the board. The Tigers didn't need it. We always drew well. But I thought it would be good for baseball, so I went along with it."

Fetzer possessed the financial means to bully his way to achieve almost any selfish interest. But his respect for organization and human dignity prevented any misuse of his wide-spread influence.

The beauty of Fetzer's financial success lies in the fact that it was literally created from nothing. He started his career armed only with imagination, initiative and a high regard for the American work ethic.

Fetzer modestly acknowledged his blessing of good fortune. He was the textbook case of how fate sometimes finds a way to gently bless a person who happens to be in the right place at the right time ... and then has the wisdom to capitalize on it.

The formula for Fetzer's success mirrored that of several other self-made pioneers of the early-to-mid-20th century. He was shrewd. He was a tireless worker. And he was brave enough to take a risk.

Fetzer chose the untested field of broadcasting even before it began to unfold. It was an industry that, at the time, literally had no history. Hardly anyone was an expert and almost all stood by quietly to marvel at just how far it might develop.

Fetzer was a true broadcast pioneer. Like the contemporary computer world, broadcasting became an industry that eventually put a stranglehold over the entire American economy. Because of its dominance over the entertainment and news-gathering operations, broadcasting—particularly television—acquired near-dictatorial power over the advertising dollar.

Even Fetzer could not have imagined television's eventual widespread power. He tip-toed modestly into the industry, literally at its birth. He marched out as one of its founding giants, leaving an imprint that still lives on today.

The power and prestige he achieved from his prominence in baseball was treated with the same modest respect he extended to broadcasting. But he certainly didn't need the game to enhance a national reputation of historical import.

"Anybody who's in baseball to make a lot of money ought to have his head examined," Fetzer said. "There is not a lot of money to be made in baseball. Baseball was far from a money-making venture for me in my business career. It has been largely a labor of love."

Fetzer's interest in broadcasting dated back to the century's first decade when he was a youngster growing up in Decatur, Indiana. Born on March 25, 1901, Fetzer was raised by his mother, the former Della Winger, after his father died when Fetzer was only two.

Fetzer was introduced to the miracle of electronic transmission when he was only ten by his brother-in-law, Fred Ribble. A telegrapher for the Wabash Railroad, Ribble constructed a crude home-made antenna and strung it between the flagpole of his Lafayette, Indiana front yard and an oak tree across the street. Working with a crystal set and a do-it-yourself headphone connection,

Ribble and a collection of family and friends were entertained by the radio broadcasts they were able to pick up from Arlington, Virginia.

It amounted to nothing but a series of dots and dashes. But it captured the fancy of its amazed audience and obviously sparked the imagination of the young John Fetzer.

Fetzer matured under the guidance of Ribble who served as the boy's surrogate father. As Ribble's interest and tinkering in this virgin field blossomed, so did Fetzer's.

The Tigers, at the time, enjoyed a considerable following in that corner of Indiana. The combination of Ribble's tinkering with this revolutionary mode of communication and the town's interest in the Tigers introduced Fetzer to the team he would eventually own.

On days of big games for the Tigers, a crowd would gather outside the railroad depot to receive updates on the latest score. Once Ribble picked it up over the wire, he summoned young John to post it on a blackboard outside the depot.

Fetzer's fascination for this new marvelous medium had been piqued. By his early teens, he began building equipment and experimenting on his own. His imagination was challenged during World War I when a moratorium on transmitting made it unwise to erect an antenna outside the family's latest home in West Lafayette, Indiana. So young John used the springs of his bed as an antenna to send messages of dots and dashes to a friend across town.

Purdue University's school of engineering had become a hotbed of developmental research in wireless telephony. Fetzer was fascinated by its limitless possibilities. Purdue was the Mecca of uncharted opportunities. At 18, he enrolled at the university.

It was at Purdue that Fetzer built his first ham radio station. He capitalized on his creation by hooking up with Dr. Frank Conrad, a Pittsburgh experimenter. The two began regular radio conversations.

From their transmissions, they discovered they had developed an audience of people living between the two cities who listened in with crystal sets. Conrad created a mild sensation when one day during a conversation with Fetzer, he played music from his phonograph over the transmission.

From their efforts, Conrad created radio station KDKA. Fetzer created WLK in Lafayette. It marked the start of a career that would last a lifetime and affect the broadcast industry forever.

Fetzer enjoyed his stay at Purdue but became restless to develop some ideas of his own. After two-and-a-half years, he left Purdue for a job as parts manager for an electrical supplier. He began building stations and consulting in the Midwest. Working in exchange for tuition so that he could complete his degree, he was asked to build a station in Berrien Springs, Michigan, for a small school called Emmanuel College (now Andrews University).

The tiny, non-commercial station thrived for a while, featuring a program of lectures and music. When the college decided it no longer could afford the upkeep, it decided to find a buyer for the station.

The asking price was $10,000. Fetzer bargained the price down to $2,500 and became a one-man operation. He personally solicited advertising. He wrote the copy, read it over the air, and also served as disc jockey. More important than all of his various duties, he served as station technician and engineer.

With a congressional debate over control of the airwaves brewing in 1925, Fetzer traveled to Europe to study the state-run broadcast systems of England, Holland, Germany and France. From there, he returned convinced that a secure free press depended on radio remaining privatized.

When the Depression struck, Fetzer looked for another city where his radio frequency would work. He settled in Kalamazoo, Michigan, which was to become his permanent home. With just a used car, his equipment and $156 in working capital, Fetzer went on the air in 1930 with a 500-watt daytime station called WKZO. During the Depression, Fetzer traded air time for meal tickets and groceries.

"I remember one time when I was flat-out broke," Fetzer recalled. "I went to see a bank official, told him who I was and what I did, and asked if I could borrow a thousand dollars. He said, 'Young man, find something else to do. There is no way that somebody can make an honest living from the air.'"

But the station flourished. It became the base of his broadcast empire. From there, his holdings blossomed. Fetzer expanded by purchasing struggling stations. He enhanced their values by adding newly developed, directional antennas. These directional antennas allowed stations assigned to the same frequency to broadcast after sunset without interfering with each other.

An Omaha, Nebraska station that shared WKZO's frequency challenged Fetzer's use of the new device. It was not until 1938, after the case had twice reached the Supreme Court, that the Senate ordered the Federal Radio Commerce (which preceded the Federal Communications Commission) to issue Fetzer the first experimental license to use the antenna. WKZO, therefore, was the first of 3,000 stations ultimately licensed under the ruling.

Fetzer's business in Washington led to a variety of friends and contacts in the federal government. He had made such an impression, in fact, that during World War II, Fetzer was appointed by President Roosevelt to serve as U.S. Censor for Radio, monitoring domestic and overseas short-wave transmissions and establishing the voluntary guidelines for what was permitted to be broadcast. Fetzer, of course, was a champion for the right of free speech. Toward the end of the war, therefore, along with other distinguished colleagues, he co-engineered the dismantling of the Office of Censorship through requests for a reduced budget. The designed reduction helped to effect the elimination of the office. The emphasis on self-regulation was Fetzer's legacy from those early battles against public control of the airwaves.

Throughout his broadcast career, Fetzer was called upon by Washington to address a variety of issues in this unfolding industry. He served as chairman of the National Association of Broadcasters' Television Code Review Board from 1952-55. He authored the television code of ethics and supervised the industry's program of self-regulation, this time for the television stations that were cropping up around the country, including his own WKZO-TV, which went on the air in 1950.

In the meantime, Fetzer continued to add to his broadcast holdings. He acquired stations in various parts of Michigan and Nebraska. In addition, he was the owner of vast amounts of land and various oil wells.

It was clear that Fetzer did not need baseball, neither for financial gain nor self-aggrandizement. The path he had chosen early in life provided plenty of both for an individual who painstakingly protected his anonymity.

But the business decision that prompted him to purchase the Tigers in 1956 also provided the opportunity for self-enrichment that can't be measured in monetary terms. It was the kind of self-enrichment that no amount of money could buy.

"I believe in baseball," Fetzer said. "I think it does have great value beyond the profit line, and I want to see it survive in the best possible shape."

Fetzer believed that baseball is good for the community. He believed it was good for youth in a manner not measurable by turnstile count. He believed in certain assets that aren't counted in dollars. For that reason, he felt that baseball must always remain vigilant to protect its special appeal.

So while Fetzer based his decision to purchase the Tigers on wise and enterprising business principles, he also seized the opportunity to enrich the game as it would him.

It was the single most satisfying reward Fetzer derived from almost three decades of baseball leadership.

And that enrichment worked both ways.

CHAPTER 5

Why the Tigers?

There are a million good reasons for wanting to buy a ballclub. There are a million and one better reasons for an entrepreneur to invest the money in a much more reliable venture.

Maybe there's no sure thing when it comes to owning any business. One guarantee about owning a ballclub, however, is that the risks are almost always greater than the financial rewards.

Buying a ballclub is generally bad business compared to an equal financial stake in a more conventional commercial opportunity. In baseball, the return on the dollar is considerably lower. The risk of losing a bundle rides merely on a few bad seasons.

"If I had gone into baseball simply to make a profit off the team, it would have been one of the most ill-advised business decisions of my career," John Fetzer said.

History proved Fetzer rarely made bad business decisions. So why did he choose to get into baseball in the first place?

Certainly the lure of the game is a potent intoxicant. It has the power to seduce some of the wealthiest businessmen. A sudden deafness to all the whistles and sirens that signal a risky business deal overcomes prospective buyers in the face of baseball temptation.

After all, baseball offers a romance that a coal company or lumber yard or almost any other type of business can't come close to matching. The game is a temptress. It entices prospects into a glamorous world where membership is limited.

Baseball is a fantasy. It seems so make-believe. Decades of comfortable anonymity can be instantly erased with the simple purchase of a major league club.

Fantasies can be dangerous, however. Owning a major league baseball team can be like walking on quicksand. It's a little boys' game dealing in big-time dollars. Even the most flamboyant eccentric sometimes gets stung in the shuffle.

Later in his career, Fetzer commented on some of the game's hidden land mines: "For every joyous moment of pompous attention you receive as owner of a major league baseball club, I can assure you that accompanying that will be at least a dozen headaches. I guess that is one of the reasons why I avoided being in the public eye as much as possible. For every moment of gladness, you seemed to have guaranteed another dozen moments of sadness."

At the time of Fetzer's entry, the Tigers featured some brilliant players. Al Kaline and Jim Bunning were two of the brightest stars. They would go on to become members of Baseball's Hall of Fame. Harvey Kuenn already had won a batting title and was one of the slickest hitters in the game. Rich or poor, what fan hasn't dreamed, at least once, about what it would be like to play owner to such real life heroes?

Fetzer's love of baseball preceded his purchase of the Tigers. He first became a Tiger fan as a boy growing up in Indiana. Like most baseball fans across the country, he followed the game closely, but hardly with a passionate zeal. Never had he entertained any romantic notion about one day owning the Tigers, or any other major league franchise for that matter.

Unlike some owners who buy their ticket to the dance for the instant celebrity that accompanies it, though, Fetzer's decision to buy the Tigers was based on a vision that would generate profit as well as provide stability to the franchise. Even before his purchase, Fetzer believed baseball shared a kindred spirit with national morality.

At the time of Fetzer's purchase, there were only 16 franchises in the major leagues. Even today, with expansion having almost doubled the number, the romance and glamour of owning a team still remains a tasty temptation.

There was one significant difference with Fetzer. He didn't need the spotlight. He accepted its obligations. But anonymity and Fetzer long had served as quite comfortable companions.

Fetzer could have had his pick of any team in professional sports. He certainly had the resources to assemble a package to buy the team of his choice. So exactly what persuaded him to select the Tigers? Why not the Yankees, White Sox, Cubs or any other club from that sweet 16?

There's no question that the glitter of the game seduced even conservative John Fetzer. There was obviously more romance to owning the Tigers than another television station or some speculative barren land somewhere in an Arizona desert.

That old English "D" on those creamy white uniforms has always cast its unique spell of magic. It was an image imprinted boldly on his imagination way back in his boyhood.

Of course, all these elements played a part in his decision to purchase. But the bottom line was business, and he made the decision believing he could blend all the romance of owning the Tigers with enhancing the strength of his expanding broadcast empire.

"Certainly, there is a fair degree of glamour attached to owning a major league baseball team," Fetzer explained. "But the truth of the matter is that we embarked on the venture of ownership as a sound business venture. Owning a major league franchise and being able to operate it in a manner so as to keep it fiscally sound are two very distinct elements. And running it in a fashion so as to maintain public trust is yet another matter."

From 1935 until Fetzer and ten other investors combined to purchase the Tigers in 1956, the team had been owned by the Briggs family. Walter O. Briggs served as sole owner until his death in 1952. He had been a leading Detroit industrialist who manufactured car bodies for the automobile companies. He purchased the team more for sporting than business interests.

Briggs tried vainly to persuade his son, Walter "Spike" Jr., to take over the manufacturing business. Spike, however, became enamored with the Tigers. After the death of the senior Briggs, the club was run by the Briggs Trust with Spike serving as president.

It was primarily during Spike's reign that the Tigers, in baseball circles, were tagged with a reputation for operating a club under loose business principles. Spike enjoyed fraternizing with the players. Dollars were spent frivolously, lavishly, and for the most part fruitlessly on the players.

The Tigers became known as the country club of the American League. Accountability to the bottom line was as foreign as a championship pennant flying over Briggs Stadium.

In 1955, the trustees of the club announced that the Tiger baseball stock was not considered a sound investment to reside in a trust where minor heirs were involved. The trustees, which included Spike's four sisters, voted to sell the club and reinvest the capital in sounder securities. The rest of that year and through the early part of 1956, Spike repeatedly attempted to put together a syndicate to buy the club, but all attempts failed. Later that year, the trustees formally announced the ground rules for the sale of the club through competitive bidding.

Carl Lee had served as top lieutenant for Fetzer's broadcast holdings. Lee also had served as president of the Michigan Association of Broadcasters (MAB). He was followed by Fred Knorr, a friend of Spike Briggs. Knorr lived in Detroit and owned radio stations around the state.

Lee and Knorr were attending an MAB meeting at the Pantlind Hotel in Grand Rapids, Michigan shortly after the Tigers had announced that the club was for sale.

"Knorr told me they were getting ready to sell the Tigers from the Briggs estate," Lee recalled. Both were interested because each had stations that carried the Tiger broadcasts. In the mid-'30s with another radio entrepreneur, George Trendle, Fetzer created a state-wide radio network to broadcast Tiger games all over Michigan. It was a lucrative package. Through the combined holdings of Fetzer and Knorr, they owned stations that covered approximately 85 percent of the state's population. Shortly after the purchase, Fetzer announced that every regular season game would be broadcast over the radio network.

Once television became popular in American households, Fetzer helped to form the Tigers' first Michigan TV network.

"In those days, the Tiger broadcasts were a pretty hot commodity," Lee explained. "We came up with the bright idea that maybe we could go to all the radio stations that carried the Tigers and see if we could put together a group to buy them."

Knorr had figured it would cost about four million dollars. Lee and Knorr initiated a call and letter campaign to solicit interest.

"We didn't do too well getting people willing to commit," Lee said. "That was big money in those days. I remember telling Knorr, 'Fred, I don't think we're going to make this thing work.' We both agreed to keep looking. It was then that I approached Mr. Fetzer with the idea."

Fetzer's first response to the availability of the Tigers was a lukewarm "So what?"At the time, he was 55 years old.

"I had always liked baseball and followed the Tigers and that sort of thing," he said. "But the last thing I wanted to do at this juncture in my life was to own a baseball team. I guess I thought I owed it to Carl (Lee) to check the thing out, so I arranged a meeting in Detroit with Knorr and Spike Briggs."

That meeting almost squashed any hope of getting Fetzer hot for the deal.

"Frankly, I wasn't too impressed with Spike," Fetzer said. "He sort of turned me off because he was a notorious drinker. He hit the 'tea' pretty heavy. So I promptly forgot the whole thing."

The attraction of owning the team for which his stations carried the broadcasts, however, remained warm in the back of Fetzer's imagination.

"I realized that if the wrong group had taken control, I might lose the rights to broadcast games," Fetzer said. "At that point, I became extremely interested. It was really an easy business decision to make because I had always been a Tiger fan."

At the 1956 national convention of American radio and television broadcasters in Chicago, Knorr tried to hook Fetzer again. Knorr convinced him that if anyone could put together a formidable enough group to buy the Tigers, it was Fetzer.

"He hooked me good," Fetzer said. "I said O.K. and not long after, I was back in Detroit meeting with Spike and Knorr's associates again. They seemed like decent fellows so I agreed to put together the syndicate, to arrange for the $250,000 bond that was required in order to check the club's books, and to enter the bidding contest for the Tigers."

Even during the creation of the syndicate, Fetzer could sense that some of the members were more enamored with the romance associated with owning a baseball team than with the "roll up your sleeves, nuts and bolts work" it took to run a club properly. While Fetzer never hid his affection for the Tigers, there was no mistaking the seriousness of his intentions.

After the sale was completed, the July 20, 1956 edition of *Newsweek* took note in a piece written by James C. Jones, the magazine's Detroit bureau chief. Jones wrote:

"The sale of a baseball club can be one of the most emotionally trying periods in the life of a sportswriter. Tears splash across their stories. Old and new owners are glamorized. Then, a day or two later, everyone is back to criticizing the team. To the 11-man syndicate that bought the Tigers, the deal was practical business. There was no sentiment involved."

The article probably was a little too harsh. Fetzer's entry into the game obviously never would have happened had it not been for his concern for the Tigers and compassion for the game.

There's no question, however, that the "bottom line" of business played a substantial role.

"My advice to anyone interested in investing in baseball is this: you'd better love it and have unlimited resources or else you'd better play with something else," Fetzer said. "Unless you are always in contention, there's no way to make it profitable."

Fetzer admired and respected the concept of disciplined business practice. He also welcomed the opportunity to nurture the warm spot in his heart that he felt for the Tigers. He was convinced that the two were compatible partners.

He promised himself to make them work together.

CHAPTER 6

Buying a Ballclub

B aseball is beautiful. The game itself embodies all the hope, life and spirit of the young. And then it keeps all of it alive to savor as we get older. It's the magic marker of memories. It's the most reliable of friends.

Between the foul lines, all the color, charm, romance and magic of wishes and make-believe come to life. The essence of the game is written on the dirt and the grass under a sizzling summer sun.

It's everything that buying a ballclub isn't.

The process of buying a team is as glamorous as a seventh-inning rain delay. It's like sitting in the stands wondering when the rain will stop. There's really nothing glitzy about a collection of lawyers, bankers and businessmen struggling to make sense out of how much a band of grown men playing a kid's game for oodles of dollars really is worth.

Fans really don't care who the new owner of their team is going to be. Not as long as there's enough pitching, a few guys who can hit enough balls over the fence to make the long summer exciting and keep the old park a special place to visit while the kids are out of school.

In the case of the Tigers, though, there are a few additional distinct conditions. Since the turn of the century, this is the team that has come to symbolize the spirit of the city.

Tiger fans, especially back in 1956, had a bleeding love affair with their boys of summer. That old English "D" represents the city's badge of honor.

There's a certain amount of intrigue surrounding the sale of any major league club. First it's generated by the mystique of baseball ownership. Then it's fed by a massive dose of media coverage that scrutinizes each minute detail.

Who will the new owner be? Will he be local? How can anyone have enough money to buy the hometown baseball team? Will the new owner share the same passion for the team as the fans who support it? Will he have a sense of the game's tradition? Will he at least know the difference between a baseball and a beachball?

While the deed to the club is held by the owner, the spirit of the team really belongs to all of its fans.

Of course, the purchase of a club entails long-term community commitments and consequences. But the actual sale, at times, requires a generous supply of "No-Doze" tablets. It's a big buck deal involving an army of gray pin-stripe suits. There's little romance to the sale of a club. The sale involves all the grueling, mundane and nondescript complexities of any big business deal. And for the most part, it is conducted behind the paneled walls of bankers' offices.

Dating back to 1901, there have been 13 ownership changes of the Tigers since hotelier and Wayne County Sheriff James D. Burns owned the club at the time of the American League charter.

In the first decade of the century, there were several changes. In 1902, insurance man Samuel F. Angus bought the franchise and hired Frank J. Navin as a bookkeeper. In 1904, William Hoover Yawkey, son and heir of William Clymer Yawkey, Michigan lumber-ore magnate, bought the franchise for $50,000. Navin was given $5,000 worth of stock and team manager Edward G. Barrow $2,500 worth of stock for arranging the deal. The next year, Yawkey bought back Barrow's interest for $1,400.

In 1907, Navin became half-owner and president of the club by paying Yawkey $40,000. That arrangement lasted until 1920 when auto industrialists Walter O. Briggs, Sr. and John Kelsey each bought 25 percent of the team from the heirs of Yawkey, who died on March 5, 1919, for $250,000 each.

That marked the beginning of the long-running Briggs' ownership. In 1927, Briggs became half-owner of the team by purchasing Kelsey's stock from his estate. In 1935, Briggs became sole owner and president when he purchased the Navin stock from his estate. Navin died November 13, 1935.

Ownership remained the same until shortly after Briggs' death on January 17, 1952. It was then that the stock was put into estate and Walter O. Briggs Jr. assumed the presidency.

The situation remained the same until all stock was sold, under court order, by all the Briggs heirs on October 1, 1956, to a syndicate of 11 radio-television men headed by John E. Fetzer, Fred A. Knorr and Kenyon Brown for $5.5 million.

In 1960, Fetzer bought out Brown and became president. On November, 14, 1961, Fetzer gave the Tigers their first sole owner since Briggs when he purchased the Knorr stock from his estate after Knorr died on December 27, 1960.

It marked the beginning of the longest run of sole ownership in Tiger history. Fetzer held the club until October 10, 1983, when he announced the sale to Tom Monaghan for a record $53 million. While Monaghan owned the club, Fetzer remained as chairman of the board for the next five years.

On August 26, 1992, Michael Ilitch purchased the team from Monaghan.

The 1956 sale of the Tigers followed fairly close to the standard script. Because it involved the Tigers, however, there were a few special twists. Those twists went with the territory of bidding for one of the most storied franchises in professional sports.

First of all, the Tigers enjoyed a unique position of prominence, not only in the city of Detroit, but also within the game.

Historians still argue that 1956 fell into baseball's golden era. It was a time of baseball brilliance when the game ruled sports as uncontested champion. It was a time of legends. A time when Mickey Mantle, Willie Mays, Ted Williams, Stan Musial and Yogi Berra became the closest figures to American royalty.

In the city of Detroit, the Tigers reigned as king. Bobby Layne's Lions enjoyed their band of diehard fans. Gordie Howe led the Red Wings in the middle of their most glorious seasons. But the Tigers were the heart of the city. Detroit was a fertile breeding ground for future major league stars. Everyone was a Tiger fan.

The Tigers are a charter member of the American League. Those long-ago players also made memories at the corner of Michigan and Trumbull. From that site, Tiger Stadium later would rise.

Tiger history is crammed with legendary figures such as Ty Cobb, Hank Greenberg, Charlie Gehringer and Mickey Cochrane. Every player to wear that old English "D" symbolized the city's pride.

So the sale of this franchise is never just another deal.

And then along came Bill Veeck. He was baseball's resident rebel, running somewhere disarmingly ahead of or disjointedly out of his time. Veeck came charging into the bidding war for the Tigers. He was never one to whisper when shouting was an option.

Veeck had been part owner of the Cleveland Indians and the former St. Louis Browns. His blood was carnival red. Ballparks under Veeck came straight out of the midway. There were fireworks and exploding scoreboards. He stunned fans and drew the ire of league officials once by sending a midget up to the plate. Veeck carved his reputation by dabbling in the bizarre. Veeck never simply slipped into a city. He charged in with trumpets blaring. There was always one more show to play.

Dressed in his trademark unbuttoned-to-the-navel Hawaiian sports shirts, Veeck called numerous press conferences and orchestrated a public spectacle while bidding for the Tigers.

There were plenty of laughs and plenty of promises. Finally the theatrics became too much to take. Even some of the local columnists were turned off by his medicine show.

"It seemed like he was holding a press conference every hour on the hour," Fetzer said. "I think he held one press conference too many."

One too many press conferences tipped the ringmaster's hand. When the decision to accept the bid of Fetzer and his syndicate was announced, Veeck screamed louder than those pre-psychedelic shirts that he fancied. Veeck called the eleven-man syndicate that purchased the Tigers in 1956 a "gang of riverboat gamblers."

Over the lives of their professional careers, each member of the group probably had been called worse by better. And even if he didn't mean it that way, coming from Veeck, it probably was a compliment.

Veeck's reference pertained to the 11th-hour daring Fetzer pulled off to seal the deal. It was like hitting a homer with two outs in the last of the ninth inning. Without those last-minute dramatics, the Tigers probably would have landed into the hands of baseball's uncontested maverick.

Working on a hunch just before the deadline, Fetzer convinced the syndicate to raise its bid for the club by a half-million dollars. That bumped the ante to a whopping $5.5 million. That's the going rate for a minor league team today. Several players at the big league level make more than that amount each year. At the time, however, no baseball club in history had ever sold for such a staggering amount. The purchase price had topped the previous record for a franchise sale by $1 million. In 1941, the New York Yankees sold for $3.4 million. The Philadelphia Phillies sold for $3.5 million when the franchise was switched to Kansas City. Brewery magnate August Busch had set the previous record of $4.5 million when he purchased the St. Louis Cardinals in 1953.

The move took guts. And it also took Fetzer to financially back a couple of members in the syndicate. But it made good business sense. It also demonstrated the insight Fetzer judiciously practiced throughout his three-decade stewardship.

The glory of sportsmanship in owning a major league baseball team is alluring. But the purchase of a franchise can't escape the nuts and bolts of good business sense. Some of it demands bravado. Some is mundane. There's no room for the timid when it comes to buying a baseball franchise.

Fetzer's purchase proved that a wisely whispered message is far more powerful than trumpets—or Bill Veeck—blaring in the wind.

After the announcement that the Tigers were for sale, eight groups joined the bidding for the storied franchise. Besides the group of Fetzer and Veeck, the others included:

—Harold Gross, a Lansing, Michigan-based broadcast owner who bid $4 million in cash.

—J.W. "Billy" Mortell, Jr., a Jackson, Michigan industrialist acting in conjunction with George "Papa Bear" Halas, the owner/coach of the National Football League's Chicago Bears. Their bid was $3.2 million in cash.

—Ray Whyte, Ozzie Olson and D. Lyle Fife, three Detroit stockholders in the Detroit Lions.

—Charles O. Finley, a Chicago-based insurance executive and later owner of the Kansas City and Oakland Athletics, and George Storer, a broadcasting entrepreneur. Initially, the pair functioned as independent purchasers. They combined their efforts shortly before submitting a final bid of $1.2 million in cash, a pledge to pay another $1.3 million in ten annual installments and a lease arrangement calling for an annual rental charge of $100,000 for the stadium with an option to buy the property at a later date for $2 million.

—Robert Goldstein, a motion picture producer from Culver City, California, along with Detroit industrialists Sidney Allen and

Max Fisher. Limited partners in the group included actor Clark Gable and motion picture director Raoul Walsh. The group offered $5 million in cash.

—Jack Kent Cooke, a Toronto publisher and radio executive who also owned the Toronto Maple Leafs Baseball Team of the International League. Part of his group included William O. DeWitt, then a New York Yankees executive, and Rudolph Schaffer, general manager of Cooke's baseball team. The bid was $3.18 million plus a $2 million land contract for buying Briggs Stadium. Cooke later went on to own the National Basketball Association's Los Angeles Lakers and then the National Football League's Washington Redskins.

—Veeck had teamed with Jerold Hoffberger, president of Baltimore's National Brewing Company, and John Hilson, president of a New York investment firm, and other limited partners. They bid $5,250,000 in cash.

Fetzer and Knorr were the key figures in the 11-man syndicate that landed the Tigers. The syndicate consisted of three groups.

Limited partners in the Fetzer group included: Carl Lee, longtime executive in Fetzer's broadcast holdings, and Paul O'Bryan, senior partner of a Washington law firm.

The Knorr group included: Harvey Hansen, owner of various lumber firms; and William McCoy, general agent for a Detroit insurance agency and secretary-treasurer of Knorr Broadcasting.

Kenyon Brown headed the third group. Brown was based in Wichita Falls, Texas and owned several radio stations in the southwest. His partners included: George Coleman, an Oklahoma banker and truck manufacturer; Joseph Thomas, partner in a New York securities firm; R. F. Woolworth, a New York securities firm expert and heir to the Woolworth dime store fortune; and movie star Bing Crosby.

Each of the groups represented one-third ownership. The syndicate's original bid was for $4.8 million. Sealed bids for the franchise were to be submitted to the Briggs trustees by midnight of July 2, 1956. The club was to be awarded to the highest bidder based upon those sealed bids.

In one of numerous press conferences that Veeck had conducted, he revealed that the National Bank of Detroit had promised him a $2.5 million line of credit.

"Our group believed that the winning bid would range between $4 and $5 million," Fetzer said. "We had obtained a line of credit from the same bank for $2 million. Based on our bid, the bank indicated this would be the maximum amount of credit it could extend to our group.

"When I read that Veeck said the same bank was offering him $2.5 million of credit, I put two-and-two together and came up with $5 million. That would have been the most ever paid for a baseball franchise up to that time.

"I got the principal members of our syndicate together. I told them I was playing a hunch, but that I was convinced I was guessing right. I told them that we should raise the ante to $5.5 million or get out of the game."

Fetzer invested more money than any of his partners in the deal. He had $1 million of his own fortune riding on the package. He also loaned O'Bryan and Brown enough to convince the group to up the ante.

The revised proposal clinched the sale. Its structure was attractive to all trustees—$4.2 million in cash, a $900,000 note payable in five years at four percent interest and a $400,000 bonus.

Veeck claimed that the revised bid had been submitted past the deadline. That was impossible, however, since all bids had been submitted in writing to the trustees.

After the winning bid was announced on July 16, Veeck raised his offer to $6 million. He later upped it to $6.75 million with deferred payments, but it was too late. The ground rules had been established and the winning bid had been selected according to prescribed measures. Veeck left town saying, "Every once in a while, a guy will be taken by a bunch of riverboat gamblers."

Along with the record $5.5 million price tag, Fetzer's winning bid carried some appealing special enticements. Not only was the majority of money coming from men of Detroit and Michigan backgrounds, but the syndicate promised to keep Spike Briggs and Harry Sisson as part of the executive team. Sisson was the longtime secretary-treasurer of the club.

Retaining the nucleus of the front office perhaps leaned the Briggs' trustees toward Fetzer's side.

Euphoria engulfed each member of the syndicate. They had just landed one of baseball's genuine gems. It was a time for celebration.

"I believe that the purchase of the Detroit Baseball Club by a group composed substantially of broadcasters doing business in Michigan, is logical and promises the best possible opportunity for promulgating the fine public service record that has been developed by the Tigers during the time of the club's ownership by the Briggs family," Fetzer said after the sale had been announced.

"Our syndicate, including Mr. Knorr and Mr. Crosby, together with their colleagues, is a group of successful businessmen in their own right. They will further strengthen the financial resources of the club and enable us to build a fine baseball organization.

"Obviously we want to run the club as a sound business enterprise, but we recognize that to do so we must reward the loyalty of Michigan's fans by giving them a winner. None of us has been identified with failure. Since we are buying a baseball team in which we have confidence, we have every reason to believe that our ultimate purpose will be achieved."

Few businessmen ever are privileged to experience the ecstasy of savoring the moment of purchasing a major league baseball team. The honeymoon was short-lived, however. Along with the normal headaches of owning a club came a stinger for which none had been adequately prepared.

Multiple ownership might work in some industries. In baseball, however, it was like a plague of sore-armed pitchers.

And it struck with the suddenness of a wicked line drive.

CHAPTER 7

The Early Years

For the most part, the second half of the '50s was more of a stroll than a mad dash into one of America's most volatile decades.

It was a crew-cut, cardigan sweater sort of era. It was a one-income family time when mom prepared dinner when dad came home from work. Shopping malls were still in the future. Groceries were purchased at the corner store. The rest of the shopping was done downtown. After dinner, the family gathered around the black-and-white box in the living room to watch shows like "I Love Lucy." Ozzie and Harriet set the standard for wholesome American family life.

Detroit at that time was one of the most vibrant cities in the Midwest. More than 1.5 million people lived within the city limits. They lived primarily in single-family homes made affordable by work within the auto industry. Suburban sprawl had yet to surface. Downtown was crammed with department stores, theaters and restaurants. It was teeming with people day and night.

And, of course, the Tigers were the darlings of Detroit.

These should have been happy days for John Fetzer and the rest of the new Tiger owners. But it wasn't until early into the next decade that Fetzer was able to smile about his ball club.

Fetzer and the syndicate did not take official control of the club until October 1, 1956. From that first day until Fetzer became sole owner more than five years later, there rarely was a calm around the old ballpark. Whether on the field or in some department distant from the dugout, the Tigers always seemed to be only one step away from another embarrassing fiasco.

The new ownership group appeared to have all the right intentions. Fetzer was named chairman of the board. Fred Knorr, because he was local, was appointed president and served on the board. Spike Briggs, son of former Owner Walter O. Briggs, was retained as executive vice president/general manager. Harry Sisson, a carryover from the Briggs regime, remained as business manager/treasurer. The four comprised an executive committee. The nine other investors were part of the board.

There was no front office purge after the purchase. On the surface, everything looked as if things were properly in place. Underneath, the pieces seemed to scatter like a doll house in a hurricane. And the main source of unrest emanated right from the top.

"We were just like all the fans," recalled Jim Campbell, who had worked for the organization since 1949. "We didn't know what to expect."

At the time of the purchase, Campbell served as business manager for the Tigers' minor league system. He later would serve as Fetzer's right-hand man in a 30-year run as Tiger boss.

"There were so many owners," Campbell continued, "it looked like most just wanted to be around a major league team. They wanted to make decisions about things they really knew nothing about. None of us knew for sure who to listen to.

"I remember telling John McHale (the director of player personnel). . . the man to watch was John Fetzer. Knorr was doing all the talking and getting all the publicity. But I could tell that Fetzer was the real power. He had this quiet command about him."

Fetzer didn't need the publicity, but suddenly, he had no choice. In the two-and-a-half months after the sale had been announced, Fetzer's life turned upside down. He had expected somewhat of a change, but he never suspected how so many years of comfortable anonymity could disappear so quickly with the simple purchase of a baseball team.

"I expected some of the exposure," Fetzer recalled, "but not that much. I never dreamed there would be such a change in my life. I quickly began to realize what it was like to live in a goldfish bowl. I wasn't ready for that. I never got used to it over the rest of my career."

Fetzer always had guarded his privacy as ferociously as a mother tiger protected her cubs. He shunned the notoriety that often accompanies wealth.

"None of us were prepared for the problems we faced," Fetzer said. "I know I wasn't. It seemed like every little move we made was scrutinized to the finest detail by the press. I didn't mind the scrutiny. But some of the guys writing these stories knew a whole lot less than anyone in our group. And none of us professed to be baseball experts."

The team the group had purchased possessed talent, including a couple of future Hall of Famers. But the Tigers had gained a rather dubious reputation throughout baseball circles. They resembled a team more from the country club than one from the American League. To the senior Briggs, the Tigers had been an expensive hobby. To his son, they had become an outright dollar-draining toy.

Money flowed frivolously and furiously; little was expected in return. For the franchise to survive the oncoming changes of the '60s, Fetzer was determined to instill sound fiscal principles without compromising the integrity of the game.

"Story after story painted a tainted picture," Fetzer recalled. "I think this evolved out of our insistence that the Detroit Baseball Company be run as a business.

"In my opinion, the mismanagement of the club had taken place prior to our ownership. What we found when we came on board were some of the best examples of bad baseball practices in the big leagues.

"Money was thrown to the winds without the slightest hesitation. The minute that budgets were installed and good management practices were inaugurated to search for proper talent, we caused considerable inconvenience to the glad-handers. They charged that we were penny-pinchers, that payments on our debt precluded us from spending money on players.

"By the end of 1960, we had spent more than $5.5 million developing new talent. That was as much as we spent for the franchise and represented more than any other club's investment in new players, including the Yankees. Saying we had bitten off more than we could chew was pure poppycock. If we were able to find one player in our farm system to help the parent club each season, we felt fortunate.

"The operation of a baseball franchise is slot machine stuff all the way. Few, if any, of the press accounts reflected any of this. They picked on our rough spots and, believe me, we had some."

The most jagged edge lay within the highest level of the organization. As Campbell had suggested, any sports team with more than one owner almost always has too many.

The glamour of owning a major league baseball team certainly can be intoxicating, especially one with the tradition and prestige of the Detroit Tigers. Fetzer undeniably appreciated that unique romantic feeling; the chance to embrace it was part of the reason he invested in the club.

Unlike his partners, however, he separated his passion for the game from the responsibilities of serving as a worthy guardian. The Tigers were one of sports' legitimate treasures. The burden of proper guardianship superseded all personal persuasions. He became alarmed at his partners' penchant for "playing" big league owner.

"It seems that in baseball, there is a very strange phenomenon," Fetzer said. "People, normally considered stable, well-balanced, good businessmen, suddenly become experts.

"Because they are fans, they think they are walking encyclopedias of baseball. Some members of that group were close personal friends. Suddenly, they considered themselves the truth, the gospel, the final word on baseball matters."

Fetzer was unconcerned with becoming an acknowledged baseball expert. He was more determined to establish the franchise as a sound fiscal endeavor. He loved his Detroit Tigers. He also realized the impending dangers if the club continued to function without a sound financial structure. The club was crying loudly for a well-conceived plan for the future.

In the hands of the real experts, Fetzer felt the actual running of the baseball operation would take care of itself. In theory, it was simple. Fetzer was to serve as chairman of the board and as somewhat of an overseer. Knorr was to make the day-to-day decisions as president. Briggs was to run the baseball activities. In actuality, however, all of the problems eventually were brought to Fetzer. None of the other partners were in a position to make major decisions.

"I was at the zenith of my career in the broadcasting business," Fetzer said. "I told the ten others that I did not want to go into baseball and have it become a distraction to the rest of my life."

It quickly became more than a distraction. Under the peering eyes of the press, the new ownership often was publicly ridiculed. Much of the criticism was the result of the owners' inability to step back and let the Tigers develop into the franchise for which it had the potential.

"They (the ten other owners) were a group of individualists, yet there was some cliquishness," Fetzer explained. "Actually during those five years (until he became sole owner), you couldn't be certain about any of the loyalties. They'd be together on one question and the next one you had no idea where they'd land.

"All of them were really good businessmen, yet they lacked maturity in how to handle baseball ownership. They were in over their heads. Suddenly, they were prima donnas. They were on a pedestal. They were news. They were being sought out by the press.

"At the beginning, they had the best of intentions. Most of the guys in the syndicate were supposedly good friends of mine, but frankly, they stumble-bummed around so much that they ended up not knowing their behinds from a hole in the ground. Because of their in-fighting and disagreeing all of the time, they were sandbagging me. Much to my own discredit, I let all of this crap go on for four years. I even had trouble in my own group. Carl Lee, of course, was no trouble. He had a small amount of stock, but it helped me control the largest block in those early days. Paul O'Bryan was a good lawyer, but he became less than a supporter as far as I was concerned."

Less than a month after the announced purchase, the group had to pay $1 million to the Briggs estate. Another $3 million was due on October 1. Because the group had to increase its bid to close the deal, more capital was required sooner than any of the partners had anticipated.

"Right then, the message should have come through to me loud and clear," Fetzer said. "This operation wasn't going to work.

"On the day we closed the deal with the Briggs estate, two partners approached me and said they hadn't come up with the necessary money to buy their portions of stock. So I guaranteed the loan of Ken Brown so he could secure what was needed from the bank. I had to do the same for Paul O'Bryan. And he was part of my group."

Fetzer also underwrote a loan to the entire syndicate when he issued a check to the National Bank of Detroit because the club's balance had fallen below the required minimum.

Stories quickly surfaced suggesting the syndicate's shaky financial stability. Rumors rapidly followed that the club again would soon be sold.

Along with his personal money, Fetzer spent plenty of valuable time refuting each rumor. The club was not for sale, but it had to clean up its operation in order to survive.

Financial speculations were just one of the problems the new owners had to face. Another embarrassing situation surfaced near the end of the 1956 season.

Upset with the team's third straight fifth-place finish, Briggs questioned Bucky Harris' managing ability in an interview with the press. Even if the new owners had agreed with their general manager, it was Fetzer's philosophy that organizational problems be handled privately behind closed doors. Sensing a change was imminent, Harris submitted his resignation, effective at the end of the season.

That set the stage for even more friction between Fetzer and the former owner whose family name still was attached to the stadium.

After an endorsement from former Tiger great and Hall of Famer Hank Greenberg, Fetzer wanted Al Lopez, who later was inducted into Baseball's Hall of Fame, to succeed Harris in 1957. Briggs decided to promote Jack Tighe from Detroit's farm system. Not wishing to undermine his general manager, Fetzer and the rest of the owners agreed upon Tighe. But friction with Briggs continued to increase.

Fetzer and several members of the syndicate fumed over publication of the group's financial package to purchase the Tigers. The information was provided candidly to the press by Knorr and Briggs.

Prior to the start of spring training in 1957, Briggs ripped into Al Kaline at a public luncheon in Detroit. Kaline, 22, who had won the American League batting title in 1955, wanted a salary boost close to the $32,000 Harvey Kuenn was earning as the highest paid Tiger.

"Kaline thinks he is another Mickey Mantle and wants more money than Mantle," Briggs said. "I don't agree and he isn't going to get it."

Briggs certainly was entitled to his opinion. But to Fetzer's way of thinking, those kinds of opinions were supposed to remain within the Tiger hierarchy, especially when Kaline admitted that he never considered himself to be as good as Mantle and wasn't trying to match the Yankee slugger's salary. It was the kind of situation that led the public to believe the new Tiger ownership was cheap.

Fetzer was also particularly disheartened by an increasing number of stories from employees about how Briggs would launch into uncontrollable temper tantrums with front office personnel.

On a visit to New York, Yankee owners Del Webb and Dan Topping met privately with Fetzer. They confided with him that he would never have an outstanding organization because Briggs was known to be "an inveterate drinker." Briggs, in fact, liked to crack jokes about never drinking until five o'clock. He would follow that line by displaying a wristwatch upon which all numbers on the dial were fives.

Briggs' fraternization with a select group of players and his public questioning of new club policies led to his inevitable dismissal from the organization.

At a meeting of the owners on April 20, 1957, Fetzer stated his belief that Briggs should be removed as general manager for not being strong enough to carry out the duties of the position. Not wishing to be part of the purging of his friend, Knorr announced his resignation as president. He was replaced by Harvey Hansen. Six days later, Briggs was fired.

Briggs had bragged about keeping an undated letter of resignation in his desk. On April 26, Fetzer and Hansen suggested he sign the letter that day.

"I never wanted to become active in baseball," Fetzer said. "Suddenly I was faced with the unsavory task of ending the Briggs era of Tiger baseball. The most difficult task for me, personally, was the firing of Spike Briggs. But it had to be done for the good of the organization."

The press again had been hand-delivered another juicy serving of dirty Tiger laundry. It was a time when Fetzer questioned himself for ever getting involved with the game.

McHale was elevated to the position of general manager. Fetzer and the rest of the group weren't so naive as to expect completely calm waters. They at least hoped this latest round of reorganization would demonstrate the deep concern they felt for the club. They made a commitment to build from within their own minor league system. Instead of gambling big dollars on older players in their declining years, the development of youth would be promoted.

The Tigers snapped their string of fifth-place finishes by slipping up to fourth in 1957. But they still ended 20 games out of first place.

Fetzer was committed to the future. He convinced his partners that all profits realized that year should be invested in the farm system.

Eventually the long-range planning would pay dividends. But there were still a lot of rocky roads to travel before everything was finally sorted out.

Before the 1958 season, McHale engineered three major trades that involved 22 players. There were plenty of new faces, but still the same results. The Tigers again finished fifth. That season is remembered more for some other significant events than the usual lack of a pennant race for the Tigers.

On June 6, Ozzie Virgil made his Tiger debut. A citizen of the Dominican Republic, Virgil is regarded as the first black ever to play for Detroit. In his home debut before 30,000 fans on June 17, Virgil collected four singles and a double.

But the consistent lack of continuity again left more stains on the Tigers. Mid-way through June, Tighe was fired as manager and replaced by Bill Norman.

The stunner, however, occurred before the Tigers left for spring training in 1959. McHale was offered and accepted the opportunity to become president of the former Milwaukee Braves. Hurriedly, Fetzer elevated Rick Ferrell to acting general manager. Campbell was put in charge of the farm system.

The Tigers finished fourth in 1959. Fetzer became increasingly concerned with the consistent mediocre finishes. He was more concerned, however, with the musical-chairs shifting of front office personnel. The instability was detrimental to building a solid foundation. Even more importantly, to the eyes of the public, the Tiger ownership continued to look like a collection of clowns.

"I couldn't blame the public for wondering what was going on," Fetzer said. "It was difficult for me to try to sort out all the moves."

Fetzer hadn't figured how to resolve the surplus of owners' problems quite yet. But he thought, at least, he had finally solved the puzzle of who should run the team from the top executive position.

His choice was career baseball executive Bill DeWitt, who was named president on November 2, 1959.

It's a good thing baseball is such a forgiving game, because this time Fetzer admittedly had to beg for pardon. DeWitt's one-year stop in Detroit was not successful.

This blunder, at least, was the catalyst to the long-term remedy the Tigers desperately needed. It would take another year of stumbling and a variety of blushing incidents. After a continuation of this comedy of errors, however, a solution would finally arrive.

CHAPTER 8

Taking Control

S ometimes, even the toughest fighter has to take a beating in a couple of rounds before punching his way to a decision.

John Fetzer took his lumps with Bill DeWitt. But at least it led to the victory necessary to lift the Tigers out of the quagmire that had made the franchise look like a re-run of the Keystone Kops. Finally, the Tigers would be on their way to the level Fetzer had envisioned from the start.

Fetzer thought he finally had put a stop to all the ridicule the Tigers were bringing onto themselves when he named DeWitt president on November 2, 1959. It took just one year for Fetzer to admit that bringing DeWitt to Detroit had been one of the biggest mistakes in his baseball career.

"It was my idea to hire him," Fetzer confessed. "I'm responsible for perhaps relying too much on the hearsay of other baseball people and for not relying on diligence and doing my own homework."

The miscasting of DeWitt, however, sparked the urgency Fetzer felt toward the unification of ownership. And so, at least in this case, the rainbow did indeed follow the storm. But what a storm! To categorize DeWitt as an enigma is like suggesting that Ted Williams was a pretty good hitter.

DeWitt had been a career baseball executive. He arrived in Detroit with rave reviews. The reviews came from a variety of sources. They came from baseball officials. They came from re-nowned members of the media. Former Yankee owner Dan Top-ping compared DeWitt to George Weiss, the architect of the old Yankee dynasty.

"When we brought in DeWitt," Fetzer recalled, "the sports-writers lavished us with bouquets. He was proclaimed the new Messiah of major league baseball in Detroit. The boys in the pressbox put their bricks away for the time being. The rookies were gone. There was a pro at the helm."

By the time he was let go one year later, the writers were close to buying DeWitt a one-way ticket out of town.

"Suddenly the oracles in the press who had proclaimed DeWitt as the Second Coming were now thrashing through their dictio-naries to find the most uncomplimentary adjectives to describe their opinions about the DeWitt regime," Fetzer said. "Never had one man become so unpopular in so short a time. For once, people in our front office agreed with the boys in the press."

Fetzer had designed a detailed organizational chart before hiring the new president. DeWitt chose to ignore the chart and assumed a role that made him appear to be sole owner of the club.

He re-designed the Tiger road uniforms . . . revamped Jim Campbell's scouting system. . . changed all personnel salary poli-cies . . . and revised the entire front office.

The office bordered on revolt when DeWitt demanded that a copy of all correspondence—regardless how mundane—must be sent to his office. It was another snowball in an avalanche of tur-moil.

Alice Sloane, who had joined the club in 1946 and remained for 47 years, exposed DeWitt's carbon-copy tactic.

"He told me: 'They think I read all of this. I just want them to think that everything that goes on in this place, I either know about or have a copy of it. I'll bet I don't read one-third of that stuff.'"

By June, Harry Sisson was ready to call it a career. Sisson was the soft-spoken treasurer and one of Fetzer's most trusted employ-ees. Fetzer was successful in talking Sisson out of leaving.

"At one time or another, I think almost everyone was going to quit if DeWitt were to remain," Fetzer said. "And that included Harry Sisson. I had to decide whether it was worth losing a trusted em-ployee like Harry for a rolling hand grenade like DeWitt."

DeWitt made his first splash the day before the 1960 season began when he traded American League batting champion Harvey

Kuenn to Cleveland for home run king Rocky Colavito. Later in the season he engineered a deal that stunned the whole game like an East Coast earthquake. He traded Manager Jimmie Dykes to the Indians for Manager Joe Gordon.

One of the beauties of baseball is that almost anything seems possible. But trading managers in mid-season is not supposed to be one of them.

"When DeWitt talked of swapping managers, I guess I kind of threw up my hands," Fetzer confessed. "By August when the bizarre switch was made, our season was over. As far as I was concerned, so was Bill DeWitt's tenure in Detroit."

DeWitt, apparently, let power consume good judgment. Dykes had become quite agitated over DeWitt barging into the clubhouse after games.

When Fetzer was made aware of the practice, his sense of tolerance was tested, too. Fetzer believed strongly that the clubhouse belonged to the manager and his players. Business matters with the general manager were to be appropriately handled upstairs. The whole affair became reminiscent of the Spike Briggs era. For Fetzer, too reminiscent!

Shortly after the 1960 season, Fetzer admitted his mistake by paying $100,000 to buy out the rest of DeWitt's three-year contract. Fetzer paid the price for violating one of his long-standing business policies of going outside the "family" to fill a critical position. It cost a lot more than money.

"With all things being equal," he once told a reporter, "whether it's in baseball or another business, I have always found it to be more advantageous in the overall picture to promote your own personnel. You are better off to have someone who is completely familiar with the system. It is costly, awfully costly, to teach new talent."

Nevertheless, the entire DeWitt experience triggered the mechanism that led to Fetzer's eventual takeover of the team that kept crying for some semblance of order.

DeWitt's firing went against the wishes of partner Kenyon Brown. Brown wanted to give DeWitt even more freedom with the club.

"One thing I had to re-establish quickly was a harmonious organization," Fetzer said. "We would flounder without one. We wanted our people to work together.

"I tried to get the point across that somebody was now in control, that the chaos of the past year would be replaced by some stability and that I wasn't afraid to admit that I had made a mistake about DeWitt. You can place a highly qualified man in a certain set of circumstances and he can prove to be 100 percent wrong. Yet, in another time, another place, he can prove himself 100 percent right.

"Sometimes you have to retreat before you can make any headway. To bring us out of the woods, it was time for a realistic, intelligent and hard-working approach to our problems. There would be no magic wands or miracles. Just initiative and lots of hard work."

That difference of opinion between Fetzer and Brown was the catalyst for a decision Fetzer had been contemplating for quite some time. Sole ownership not only would make the operation of the club smoother, it had become a necessity.

On October 11, 1960, Fetzer bought the Brown group out of the syndicate for almost $900,000. He now held two-thirds of the stock and had the clout to call all the shots.

At that time, Fetzer was prepared to make a clean sweep. An offer to buy out all of the Knorr Tiger stock was rejected. Persistence paid off. One year later, the deal would be complete.

"When we (the syndicate) would get behind those closed doors of the board meeting room, all hell would break loose," Fetzer said. "Those friendly guys could become vicious. There wasn't yelling or screaming, just a lot of politicking and jockeying for position to see which one could emerge as the strong man. There was all kinds of politics to unseat Knorr as the first president. One or two of them always seemed to be leaking stories to the press. Frankly, I got sick and tired of it. That's when I started thinking about buying all of them out."

With Gordon having resigned as manager the day after the 1960 season ended before DeWitt could fire him, Fetzer hired Bob Scheffing to manage the club in 1961. The Tigers made a strong bid to bring Casey Stengel back out of retirement. But the legendary Hall of Famer wound up with the expansion New York Mets.

With Norm Cash winning the batting title, the Tigers made a legitimate run for the pennant in 1961. They were in second place by only one and one-half games as they entered a Labor Day showdown with the Yankees. The Tigers were swept and finished eight games behind the Yanks in spite of winning 101 games.

Knorr, sadly, witnessed nothing of the unexpected Tiger run. While vacationing in Fort Lauderdale the previous winter, he suffered serious injuries when he slipped in a bathtub. On December 27, 1960, he died from the bizarre accident after two weeks on the critical list.

Fetzer negotiated with Knorr's estate to purchase the final one-third of Tiger stock. On November 14, 1961, the deal was finally settled for $2 million.

For the first time since Walter Briggs, Sr. had died in 1952, the Tigers were under the direction of a sole owner—John Fetzer.

For the good of the franchise and the good of the game, Fetzer believed the deal had to be done. As he painfully had to admit, under the umbrella of 11 individual owners, the Tigers had become "the laughing stock of the city . . . the league . . . and the game."

"Baseball had become so complicated," Fetzer said, "that it was extremely difficult to administer the affairs by group ownership. The complexity would only grow over the next 20 years.

"I had learned that a team should be run by one individual who had the authority to make decisions and carry them out. It cost me a lot of money and a lot of blood to finally figure that out."

Nevertheless, the mish-mash of group ownership finally was finished. Fetzer now had the opportunity to enhance a Tiger image that had unfortunately been blemished.

"You could sense when Mr. Fetzer bought out the Brown group and had majority control that somehow the Tigers were going to get on the right track," Campbell said.

"Then, when the Knorr interests were out of the picture, he had a meeting with all of us. He said that we were going to rebuild this organization, rebuild it from within and rebuild it the right way from the bottom up. He brought stability to the organization, put it on an even keel. We didn't overhaul the personnel. We just changed the mechanics of operating and had a purpose. We stayed on course the rest of the way."

Fetzer made a promise. He made it to himself and to all Tiger fans. He vowed never to allow the mismanagement of the Tigers he had witnessed to recur for as long as his stewardship should last.

He kept that promise by molding the Tigers into one of the most highly respected franchises in professional sports. When he finally sold the club 21 years later, he turned over a debt-free, healthy franchise to his hand-picked successor.

Appropriately, the Tigers captured a World Championship in their first year of ownership of Tom Monoghan.

After a few years, Monaghan encountered financial problems that forced him to sell the team. But he had begun with an operation that was regarded as one of the finest franchises in professional sports. All the derisive laughing had ended more than two decades prior to the championship of 1984.

CHAPTER 9

The Odd Couple

Years ago, when kids played pick-up games on the sand-lots, rarely were there real bases. First, second and third base often were rocks or empty tin cans. Home plate was an old sheet of newspaper held down by a sprinkling of stones.

Most of the time there weren't enough kids for nine on a team, so anything hit to the right of second base usually didn't count. Without a first baseman, the ball fired to the pitcher's hand counted as an out.

Conditions weren't always perfect. But kids were good at making the game work. When there were nine on a side on a real diamond, though, the time was special. It was baseball at its best. Everyone wished it could be like that all the time.

The same sort of principle applied to John Fetzer and Jim Campbell. Without Campbell, Fetzer would have been successful in baseball. With him, however, both left a mark on the game that is worthy of Hall of Fame consideration.

There is no better way to appreciate Fetzer's entire approach to baseball than to understand Jim Campbell. It can be argued, in fact, that without Campbell, Fetzer would not have enjoyed the success he did in the game. And Campbell, without Fetzer, never would have had the opportunity to grow into the character he did.

"Throughout my whole career, I have never seen a better match than Mr. Fetzer and Jim Campbell," said lifelong baseball executive and former American League President Lee MacPhail.

"Both were men of unimpeachable integrity. Both were concerned with the good of the Tigers and the long-term good of the game. They were part of history. Together, they wrote history. I'm not sure we'll witness that type of mutual loyalty in the game ever again."

On the surface, Fetzer and Campbell were about as much alike as a fastball and a knuckler.

Fetzer stood about six-feet, two-inches. Even in his advancing years, his weight never appeared to vary. He always looked physically fit. His gray hair, though thinning, was neatly combed straight back and never out of place. He wore conservative dark suits or sports coats. Rarely was he seen without the precise subtle necktie. There was a distinguished ambassadorial presence about Fetzer.

Campbell was almost a half-foot shorter than Fetzer. He had a roly-poly build and never let one of his monthly diets interfere with a good steak or a between-meals snack. Early in his career, he enjoyed an occasional scotch and water. After giving up cigarettes, he appreciated a good cigar. For health purposes, he eventually abandoned all drinking and smoking. Except for seafood, to which he was allergic, he never encountered a meal that he really didn't like.

Campbell was prematurely bald. Gray hair lined each side of his head. He was more of a sportscoat and slacks than a full suit sort of guy. He owned drawers full of Countess Mara neckties but usually wore one of a handful of favorites that featured red. A business graduate of Ohio State University, Campbell was bright and methodical. His speech and cordiality always reflected his working-class upbringing in Huron, Ohio, located on the banks of Lake Erie, not far from Cleveland.

He quickly corrected anyone who referred to him as "Mr. Campbell." He insisted upon "Jim."

While Fetzer always remained the perfect picture of serenity, Campbell was much more animated. He asked direct questions. He gave straight answers. No one walked away from Campbell ever wondering what he meant. He could be brusque. And he wore his emotions on his sleeve according to the fortunes of the Tigers. He always was honest and put the team ahead of everything else in his life.

Strictly from physical appearance, the two seemed as similar as Bowie Kuhn's and Marvin Miller's approach to player free agency. Inside, however, they shared an equal passion for baseball and an appreciation of sound, ethical business practices. Their spirit was so similar that it is likely never to be matched so perfectly in baseball again.

Fetzer's life was speckled with some of baseball's most historical figures. Even today their names trigger flashbacks to a time acknowledged as baseball's "golden age."

Mickey Mantle, Ted Williams, Willie Mays, Yogi Berra. Even the owners—Walter O'Malley, Tom Yawkey, Phil Wrigley, Calvin Griffith, John Galbreath — evoked a special magic of their own.

There were unforgettable characters on the Tigers. Some enjoyed lifetime careers. Others struck and disappeared with the flash of a single miracle season. Sparky Anderson, Billy Martin, Al Kaline, Denny McLain, Mark "The Bird" Fidrych.

All in their own way—some good, some not so good—left an indelible mark on the Tigers, their fans and the game forever.

From this entire cast of characters, none was more significant to Fetzer than Jim Campbell—often respectfully referred to as "The Buddha" because of his shiny top and beer barrel middle.

Campbell now is a baseball dinosaur. He spent his entire 43-year career working for the Tigers. For 30 years he ran the entire organization either as general manager or chief executive officer. That's a major league record and constitutes about 30 percent of the Tigers' American League history, which dates back to the charter year of 1901.

Because of the way the game has evolved, a run like his will never be duplicated. He was easily one of the most respected executives the game has ever produced.

"Jim Campbell was truly a singular character in the baseball sense," said former Commissioner Bowie Kuhn. "Baseball needs singular characters like him and he's a fine example.

"He was the old-style type of general manager. There was a certain gruffness on the outside that covered up the heart of gold.

"He had a great fundamental knowledge of the game. He didn't have to look in the rule book. He knew what was in the rule book. He had an absolute love of baseball. He grew up in baseball. He had this sense about him like 'You can't do anything bad to baseball.'"

Campbell, indeed, was a throwback to the game's golden age of general managers. The great ones became almost as well known as some of the players they controlled.

There was George Weiss, architect of the Yankee dynasty. Buzzie Bavasi, boss of the Dodgers. The father-son-grandson line of the MacPhail family. All enjoy a unique stature in baseball history.

They operated during a time when the general manager was "the main man." They were responsible for overseeing the entire franchise. They signed and traded the players. They set the price of the hot dogs that were sold in the stands. They decided which games would be televised. They called all the shots.

"The relationship between Mr. Fetzer and Jim Campbell is hard to explain if you didn't see it for yourself," said Hall of Fame Tiger Al Kaline. "Mr. Fetzer gave Jim complete control. I don't think we'll ever see anything like that again. The game has gotten so big."

Jack Tighe was even more emphatic. Tighe's 54-year tenure with the Tigers may be a major league record. He was the stereotypical grizzled baseball lifer. Under the leather exterior, though, he had the softness of baby powder. He also possessed the insight of a wizened philosopher.

"Never, never, never," Tighe answered when asked if baseball would ever again witness a relationship such as the one shared by his two bosses.

"Jim Campbell was such an honest S.O.B. Mr. Fetzer was able to trust him with his deepest secrets and Campbell could do the same with him.

"It was the damnedest thing you ever saw. Campbell was so loyal to Mr. Fetzer that it sort of set up a similar line of loyalty of employees to Campbell. It kind of spread throughout the whole organization. It was easy then for Mr. Fetzer to be so loyal to everyone because of the way all of the employees felt toward Campbell."

Tighe and Campbell were roommates at Buffalo, Detroit's minor league affiliate, in 1952. Tighe managed the team and Campbell served as business manager. Years later, after Campbell had become the Tiger general manager, Tighe had the opportunity to join the old Milwaukee Braves as director of player personnel.

"Frank Lane was running the Milwaukee club," Tighe recalled. "He offered to double my salary. I can't explain it, but I just couldn't make the move. I felt this tremendous loyalty to Mr. Fetzer and Campbell.

"Later, when Lane talked to Campbell, he asked him; 'What the hell is going on there? You guys must be queer or something. I offered your man twice the money he was making and he told me he couldn't leave.'

"That's the kind of loyalty that was created by Mr. Fetzer and Campbell. They were two beautiful roses off the same bush."

Loyalty and honesty are two words used often to describe Campbell.

"I went to work for the Detroit Tigers because of one man— Jim Campbell," explained former Manager Sparky Anderson. "And I stayed with the Tigers because of one man—Jim Campbell.

"I didn't know Mr. Fetzer when I first went to Detroit. But I knew that if Jim thought so highly of him, then he had to be a helluva guy. Jim told me I would never have the opportunity to work for an owner as good as Mr. Fetzer. And he was 100 percent right.

"I know this doesn't sound politically correct right now, but Jim was a man's man. If he told you something, then you could take it to the bank. He never messed around with anyone's business. He let you go out and do your job. When it came to loyalty, there wasn't anyone ever in the game who had more. If he was your friend, then he was your friend for life. And you were a lucky man for it."

Anderson proved how much he trusted his friend when it came to contract negotiations.

"There were none," Anderson said. "We'd talk a little. He'd ask what I wanted . . . what I thought was fair. A few days later he'd come back with a contract. I'd ask him, 'Is everything we talked about in there?' He'd say, 'It's all here.' I'd pick up the pen and sign it. That's how much I trusted him. He wasn't going to lie to me. He wasn't going to cheat. He didn't know how to. When Jim Campbell gave his word, it was like the tablets that Moses brought down from the mountain."

The Fetzer/Campbell situation was special for a variety of reasons. One is that even though they traveled different routes to get where they did in baseball, they arrived at the same destination.

Campbell worked for the Tigers before Fetzer bought into the franchise. Born in Huron, Ohio, in 1924, Campbell spent three-and-a-half years (1943-46) in the Navy Air Corps. Following his discharge, he returned to Ohio State University and played baseball for the Buckeyes.

In 1949, he was hired by the Tiger organization as business manager of the Thomasville, Georgia, farm club. The first night on the job, the ball park burned down.

"I thought that was it for me," Campbell laughed later.

Of course, history proved that was the furthest thing from the truth. He made various other minor league stops before being called to Detroit after the 1952 season to serve as business manager of the entire farm system. One of his proudest accomplishments was overseeing the construction of Tigertown, the Tigers' minor league complex which houses spring training in Lakeland, Florida. Even today it is regarded as one of the finest facilities in the game.

After serving 16 years as general manager, Campbell was named president in 1978. He later served as chairman of the board after Fetzer sold the club to Tom Monaghan.

In the Fetzer era, general managers were known as baseball "lifers." They weren't lawyers. They weren't manipulators of the modern marketing mystique. They were simply "baseball men." Deals were made on the strength of a handshake. It was a time in baseball when nothing was more iron clad than a man's word.

The reliability of Campbell's handshake was known in baseball circles to be an indelible mark. Campbell's word was far more solid than any document contrived by the highest priced battery of lawyers. Contracts have loopholes. Campbell's word was sacred.

Campbell not only was admired by his baseball peers, he also commanded the respect of an often abrasive media. The media was not always complimentary toward him. It often charged him with being too frugal with Fetzer's money. But all respected his honesty, work ethic and courage to stand behind his convictions even in the face of an avalanche of second guessing.

Campbell never dodged an issue with the media. He gave straight and simple answers even to the toughest questions. They weren't always what the media wanted to hear, but the media never walked away empty-handed or wondering what he meant.

Equally important in Campbell's dealings with the media was his availability. He was always around. Day or night. He returned every phone call. It was not unusual for Campbell to place a few calls of his own to the media when he was upset with the coverage of his Tigers.

Campbell's rapport with the media was not restricted to the Detroit market. Out of town baseball writers loved working with him. His accessibility was limitless compared to what many became used to in their own home cities. As long as the subject was baseball, Campbell didn't keep a meter on how long he would talk.

Campbell may not have always liked what the media wrote and reported. But he never ducked anyone. He never betrayed a confidence. He knew how to play the members of the baseball media like a gold glove shortstop.

Campbell not only loved the game, but also was fearless in his defense of it. He was possessed by doing what was right for the Tigers and baseball overall. His decisions weren't always popular; some of them invited biting criticism from both the media and the fans.

But he stood behind his convictions. Once he made a decision, he never cowered in its defense.

Before a home night game in 1973, for instance, Campbell was hit by an unexpected curveball. Dick McAuliffe, the popular long-time second baseman, visited the general manager in his office and asked to renegotiate his contract or else he would retire from the game.

"He said he wanted more money and he wanted it right now," Campbell recalled. "He said he would give me until the game was over to make any necessary calls. If he didn't get it, he was quitting baseball that night.

"I told him it wasn't necessary for me to make any calls. I said I would give him my answer right now, and that was no."

The Tigers had long employed a club policy that prohibited contract renegotiation during a season unless it had been agreed to when the deal was originally signed.

"I told Dick that I was shocked and disappointed, and that in my opinion, he was actually blackmailing me and the Detroit Baseball Club," Campbell added.

After McAuliffe left the park, Manager Billy Martin, Coach Dick Tracewski and Shortstop Eddie Brinkman called him at home to try to persuade him to return.

"Shortly before game time, I called Dick," Campbell said. "I told him in plain, simple terms that I was very deeply hurt and shocked by his actions. I told him that in my opinion, he was making the greatest mistake of his life."

Campbell, indeed, had been hurt. But he refused to surrender to something he did not believe in, even if it involved a long-time favorite like McAuliffe.

McAuliffe told Campbell that he would think things over. He was 20 minutes late, but he returned to the park for the game.

"He called me the next day from Chicago to apologize," Campbell said. "He told me that he felt two inches tall. I told him to forget the whole thing and just go out and play ball."

Campbell could be gruff, but he had the ability to deal with anyone. And he would work over the most trying conditions as long as it was for the good of the Tigers. He proved that during the nearly three-year stay of Billy Martin as manager.

"What baseball people weren't used to was the marriage between Jim and Billy," Fetzer said. "It was Jim's idea to hire him. They were so different in their ways. Billy fired from the hip, shooting first and asking questions later. Jim was a cool, conservative, logical customer.

"Billy couldn't stand to be criticized, while Jim's hide had been flayed in the sports pages. He didn't relish the hatchet jobs, but he accepted it as part of the job."

So even though Campbell didn't necessarily agree with all of Martin's methods, he allowed the fiery manager to do his job. Until some of those methods trespassed the rules—both written and unwritten—of the game.

When it came to that kind of transgression, Campbell drew the line. Although he was heaped with a mountain of criticism from the fans, he knew that dismissing Martin was the right thing to do. It was his decision and he never backed down.

In the time of Fetzer's ownership, the general manager ran the entire franchise. Picking the right G.M. was as critical to an organization as signing the right prospects.

The recipe for the successful general manager was simple. He needed a healthy dose of administrative skills, a somewhat indefinable feel for the game, the ability to put all the right pieces together, and just enough guts to take a chance when all odds appeared to be against a particular move.

Fetzer felt he finally had landed his prize when he hired Bill DeWitt after the 1959 season. DeWitt certainly had a nose for the game. He came highly recommended by Fetzer's peers and a select number of the national press. But DeWitt's obtrusive personality almost single-handedly destroyed an entire front office. He ran the club with a tyrannical fist. For the good of the organization, he had to be replaced.

Fetzer was stunned by the DeWitt debacle. It took just one disastrous and forgettable season to admit his mistake. He quickly elevated long-time executive Rick Ferrell on an interim basis to succeed DeWitt. But Fetzer was intent on finding the long-range solution.

"In all honesty, Mr. Fetzer chose Jim because he already was there and knew the entire organization from top to bottom," said long-time Fetzer confidant Carl Lee. "Jim probably was a little younger and less experienced than Mr. Fetzer ideally had wanted. But he decided to take the chance. It turned out to be the best decision he ever made for the club."

Campbell was vice president of the Tigers' minor league system and scouting, serving as Ferrell's right-hand man at the time of his promotion. At the end of the 1962 season, Fetzer elevated the 38-year-old Campbell to general manager. It was a time when any baseball executive under the age of 40 was considered to be just a greenhorn learning the intricacies of the game.

"To be honest, when I elevated Rick Ferrell to succeed DeWitt, I thought Jim was about ten years away from being able to run a club," Fetzer said. "But he demonstrated an ability to take charge. He knew our whole system. He knew the game. And more than anything else, Jim Campbell probably was the most honest man I had ever encountered."

No baseball executive in history enjoyed the longevity and respect of his peers as did Campbell. His counsel and expertise were valued not only by the league offices but also by every club in both leagues.

More than once there was a move to persuade Campbell to accept the presidency of the American League. His name also was mentioned as a candidate for Commissioner. Campbell, instead, preferred to remain with the organization for which he served his entire professional career.

One of the reasons for the remarkable Fetzer/Campbell relationship was that both believed the game represented the highest ideals of mankind. Both also believed that organization and hard work were the only means to reach the game's highest standards.

Campbell was not a rubber stamp extension of Fetzer. He was, rather, a tireless administrator and hopeless baseball romantic.

"I can honestly say that in all my years of working for Mr. Fetzer, we never exchanged cross words," Campbell said. "We had disagreements where both of us would exchange our opinions, but they were productive. That's the way it's supposed to be.

"Mr. Fetzer never professed to be a baseball expert. He left that for the professionals. But he had an uncanny way of looking at all sides of an issue. He usually came up with something that none of us had thought about. He never forced his opinion down our throats. He'd merely say: 'It looks like you've done your home-work, but have you looked at it this way?'

"When he said something like that, I normally would say: 'You've got a point, Mr. Fetzer. Maybe we should try it.' Usually, he was right, though. And besides, Mrs. Campbell didn't raise a fool."

Campbell was the perfect choice to run Fetzer's baseball in-terests for a variety of reasons:

—Campbell provided Fetzer a daily presence with the Tigers so that the owner could focus on industry-wide issues, along with overseeing his broadcast interests from Kalamazoo, Michigan.

—Both believed in the tradition of creating a winner from within the organization. A long-range successful franchise is one that develops talent from within its minor league system.

—Both believed in longevity. Fetzer never entertained selling the club until an advanced age. Campbell never entertained the idea of leaving the Tigers for any other position.

—Neither believed that owning a baseball team was a "get-rich-quick" gimmick. Fetzer charged Campbell with breaking even financially each season. Campbell responded by turning at least a small profit during each year of his leadership.

—Campbell had a solid business background and was expert in the intricacies of baseball operations.

—Campbell also developed a national reputation that brought prominence to the Tigers in all league affairs.

—Campbell had a work ethic second to none in the game. He was known to work every day of the year, including Christmas and New Year's.

—More significant than any quality, however, was Campbell's loyalty to the Tigers and the game.

"I don't know exactly what you would call it, but there was a natural compatibility between Jim's outlook and mine," Fetzer said. "We normally saw just about everything alike and drew the same conclusions.

"And from his personal being, I never had any executive in any of my companies that had the innate loyalty that Jim always displayed. There was never a more loyal person to come down the line."

Campbell's loyalty was rewarded by an authority that made his reign almost autonomous. From outward appearances, it looked as if Campbell actually owned the club.

"It was a unique kind of relationship," said former Tiger and Hall of Famer George Kell. "It was something like a guy going to Europe for a year and turning over the keys to his house and the deed to his business and saying to a friend, 'Here, you take over till I come back.' That's the kind of trust Mr. Fetzer had in Jim. And Jim never betrayed it."

The unique relationship allowed the Tigers the luxury of keeping potentially complicated matters untangled.

"I was entrusted to make decisions that other guys might have had to go through all kinds of committees for," Campbell said. "Certainly on the big issues, I'd talk to Mr. Fetzer first. And I kept him informed on everything we did."

Campbell did this through daily telephone calls regardless what part of the world Fetzer may be in.

"Sometimes the overseas calls were tricky," Campbell said. "I'd get up at all hours in the middle of the night. Sometimes it was just a briefing of what had happened on a particular day. Other times there were critical matters to deal with. That's why I used to get so upset when I'd read somewhere about Mr. Fetzer being an absentee owner. That was a bunch of unadulterated bunk. He was closer to the operation than a lot of owners who sat behind a desk everyday."

Campbell's devotion to the Tigers even superseded his personal life. After the Tigers won the World Series in 1968, Helene, his wife of ten years, demanded that he choose between her and baseball. Campbell's choice, of course, was obvious. He never re-married.

Each winter, the day before spring exhibition games began, Campbell was known to repeat the same line: "Tomorrow is the most important day of the year. Starting tomorrow and every day the rest of the season, there'll be at least one boxscore to read in the paper."

For Campbell, that was a serious matter.

"I was blessed with the way Mr. Fetzer chose to run the Tigers," Campbell said. "Serving more than one owner simply doesn't work. It's impossible to get anything done in baseball when you have to deal with more than one owner. Things happen too quickly. Waiting for a committee to make a simple decision can blow your chances of getting anything done.

"I'm grateful for the confidence Mr. Fetzer always demonstrated in my decisions. We always felt we were a step ahead of everyone else because we shared that confidence in each other."

The loyalty that Campbell demonstrated to Fetzer certainly was extended in return. While Campbell handled the day-to-day operation of the Tigers, Fetzer was free to devote his insight to the future of the game.

It was a taxing undertaking and demanded more energy with each passing season. And without Campbell, it may have been a task too great even for Fetzer.

CHAPTER 10

The Right Way

I n three decades of Tiger ownership, John Fetzer's visits to the clubhouse could be counted on one hand.

Much to the discomfort of the players, some contemporary owners make the clubhouse a regular stop. Some escort members of the family to the clubhouse. Others take friends or business associates on tours. Maybe they feel it's part of the privilege for buying into the game. Maybe the mystique of mingling with the players is a temptation too great to resist.

Fetzer loved his players. Those who stuck with the Tigers for any length of time were regarded almost as family.

But he was unbendable with a few unwritten rules of ownership. And mixing regularly with players was definitely against those rules. For Fetzer, the clubhouse was a place where players conducted their own business. Under the manager, the clubhouse belonged to them. Except for very special circumstances, the business conducted in that clubhouse was none of the owner's affair.

Two memorable moments demanded that Fetzer break his self-imposed rule prohibiting him from entering the players' turf. One came on October 10, 1968 after the Tigers had rallied from a three games-to-one deficit to win the World Series over the St. Louis Cardinals. Sixteen years later on October 14, Fetzer again made one of his rare visits to congratulate his boys after the Tigers marched through the San Diego Padres in five games to capture another world championship. The celebration was delirious and raucous.

"They were rowdy times," Fetzer recalled. "But it was a celebratory rowdyism that was beautiful in spirit."

Over the years it would have been easy for Fetzer to look the other way when it came to his rule about visiting the clubhouse. At least once in a while, perhaps as a special favor for a relative or a valued business associate. But Fetzer believed the bending of any rule reveals a lack of discipline. A relaxation of discipline from the top often creates ripples throughout an entire organization.

"There was a great sense of orderliness about John Fetzer," said former Baseball Commissioner Bowie Kuhn. "Orderliness meant you had an organization. John was the chair. Jim Campbell was the general manager. And the manager led the players. Everybody had a job and they all worked for the team. They didn't work for themselves. They weren't individual contractors. That's a tremendous tribute to John."

Fetzer ran all of his businesses—and his life—according to a fairly simple set of principles—hard work, orderliness, loyalty, and a sense of tradition. He believed in those disciplines. He practiced them without variation. It was the perfect philosophy to bring to baseball. It was a time when the game, and not all of the current peripheral activity, was what mattered most.

From its very beginning, one of the most universally appealing beauties of baseball was its simplicity of spirit. Everyone knew the rules. The purpose was obvious, like a trot around the bases after hitting a ball over the fence.

First as youngsters, the game invited us all to join. There was no restriction on size. None on gender. Everyone was welcome to get dirty in an old-fashioned game of hardball. Diamonds were carved out of empty patches of grass. Sometimes a vacant parking lot or an alley was a good enough place to pick up teams.

Later as spectators, once our old gloves were put to rest, we savored memories and the reassurance that the game would remain the same.

Over the years, baseball used that simplicity as a badge of honor. It lifted the game above the level of sport. Regardless how tangled and twisted modern society became, the purity of the game remained a trusted constant. Through wars, depression and the sometimes muddled messes of everyday life, we learned to rely upon that simplicity of baseball. It always was there. And that was good enough.

As simple as the game was on the field, it remained pretty much the same behind the scenes of major league baseball. Trying to make all the pieces fit together was a jigsaw puzzle played for keeps by the general managers. Fans made their own make-believe moves as they followed the fortunes of their favorite teams.

Of course, there were the usual problems of trying to win on the field while maintaining a fiscally sound franchise so that all the bills were paid on time.

But the simplicity of the game projected a sense of sportsmanship over business. There was an unwritten shared sense of honor among owners. Above all else, the game was the only thing. Fetzer embraced that spiritual essence of simplicity. He defended its existence. He fought for its maintenance.

Because Fetzer never compromised his principles with any matter pertaining to baseball, the operation of the Tigers reflected his overall approach to the game. In a 1980 speech delivered to the Outlook Club in his hometown of Kalamazoo, Michigan, Fetzer detailed the essence of his ownership.

"How you win must become equally important to winning at any price," Fetzer said. "Greed, ego-mandering, undercutting, and selfish self-centering for the sake of aggrandizement are far too prevalent. Too often these characteristics prevail over the public interest. Some owners are in the game to elevate their profiles and attract national prominence. These are the fellows who will spend millions to buy a winner. They wear their championship rings and blow smoke from their cigars in the face of the world.

"It is anticipated that there will be continued turnover in ownership. There is only one ownership remaining today in the American League that was there when I came in almost a quarter of a century ago. I have seen 48 different owners come and go. I have watched new owners come in with 'Messiah' complexes. For the most part, they generally come in swinging only to find out that the normal rules of business do not apply to this strange environment. As a matter of fact, every time a new, inexperienced owner comes in to take over the helm of a club, it's almost tantamount to that of placing a machine gun in the hands of a baby."

Accordingly, Fetzer ran the Tigers under sound and simple business principles. Always, he took great care to operate under the basic premise that no team or no individual was more important than the overall health of the game.

"From the standpoint of financial gain, I could think of any number of businesses that rank higher in stability and predictability of your return on investment than baseball," Fetzer said. "Most are vastly superior to anything you can attain in baseball.

Fetzer fully embraced this approach to the game. He believed the intangible value of baseball traveled far beyond the normal parameters of profit and loss.

"In baseball, you are dealing with the human equation," he said. "If you can't manage people, you are not going to succeed. For the Tigers to be successful, the franchise had to be run like a well-organized business, not a country club. Nobody believed me when I said that the Detroit Tigers were a public trust, a part of the fabric of the community. The team must not and should not be an ego trip for the owner, nor for the ballplayers, for that matter."

Because Fetzer recognized baseball's unique essence, he was easily able to appreciate the game from the vantage point of the average fan.

"Baseball was never in the big business class of General Motors or Occidental Petroleum or some of the other giant companies," he explained. "But it had all of the headaches of big business. There were the same tax laws, inflation, labor unions, contracts, the Sherman anti-trust laws, and the economic condition of the nation. A baseball owner had to live the life of a riverboat gambler because he could either make a lot of money or lose a lot in one year. You had to learn to live with that.

"I looked at my involvement with baseball as a love of accomplishment more than just a monetary reward. From that standpoint, I was not the average businessman. I have never been interested in money, per se, which I know some people will find very hard to believe. I always believed in producing a better product. If that happens, then money becomes the residual result."

The difference between Fetzer and most of the present owners is that he adhered to baseball's traditional method of developing a winner. He believed that the most meaningful product was one that was built from within the system. He initiated that program when he first assumed complete control after the 1961 season. In spite of sometimes voracious public criticism, he never wavered throughout his career.

"We adopted the slogan inside our shop that our principal business would be to build," Fetzer once explained to the media. "It's been amply demonstrated that you can't go out and buy a championship."

Even if it were possible to purchase all the players necessary to make a run at the pennant, there is no guarantee of victory. And if victory were to happen, the result would seem somewhat hollow. It's like throwing yourself a birthday party because none of your friends really care.

The process of player development contributes significantly to the reward of fulfillment. It also helps to establish a bond between the players and fans.

Development of a sound baseball organization is not limited to the players on the field. It starts, in fact, with securing the best front office administration.

"I have always maintained that unless teamwork starts at the top, it never will show itself on the playing field," Fetzer said.

And teamwork, for Fetzer, was a reflection of unity.

"Acknowledgment of the achievements of the other fellow can only improve the estimate of your own stature," Fetzer once told his employees. "I think all of us agree that in baseball there is far too much grabbing the limelight in a maddening competition for ink."

Fetzer's philosophy for operating the team, consequently, was based on three basic premises:

—Stay competitive.

—Build from within the organization.

—Don't lose money in the process.

"It sounds simple, but that's the way he ran the Tigers," said lifelong executive Jim Campbell.

"Once Mr. Fetzer took over the team, there never was a crossover from any of his other businesses. He ran the Tigers independently of all his other interests. He established a separate set of standards by which to run the team.

"He never told me I had to make a certain amount of profit one year and a certain amount another. There were plenty of better ways for Mr. Fetzer to make money. Baseball isn't the kind of business that turns out huge profits. It takes too much money to run a club properly and the risks are too great. He wasn't in it to make money. All he ever told me was not to lose money."

Lifelong baseball executive and former American League President Lee MacPhail concurred.

"I was privileged to know Mr. Fetzer for almost his entire career in baseball," MacPhail said. "I never once heard him refer to making a profit to serve as the motive for his being in the game. He simply loved baseball and tried very hard to make it better."

Fetzer's original interest in purchasing the Tigers was, in part, influenced on a business decision to ensure broadcasting rights for his radio stations. Once part of baseball, however, he surrendered his spirit to the passion he had felt for the game ever since his youth.

With Fetzer, the game was always "the thing." There was a place for promotions and marketing. But never at the expense of baseball. He was at the forefront of baseball innovation as long as any proposed revision did not tinker with the essence of the game.

"We ran our share of promotions," Campbell said. "We had Bat Day and Ball Day and a few of those basic types of events. But they were secondary. The ballpark wasn't going to turn into a carnival. Baseball always took top billing at Tiger Stadium. The best promotion—and Mr. Fetzer always agreed—was watching a winning team on the field. Isn't it funny how winning teams always seem to draw the most people?"

The Tigers did their share of winning. In 27 years under Fetzer ownership, the Tigers played under .500 only eight times. From 1962 through 1983 when he served as sole owner, the Tigers posted a record of 1818-1681. During the five years (1984-1988) he served as chairman of the board after selling the club to Tom Monaghan, the Tigers went 461-348.

"Here's why Mr. Fetzer was such a good owner for baseball," Campbell explained. "He wasn't like a lot of owners who make all kinds of noise talking about how he was going to win all the time. That doesn't happen in baseball.

"He was patient. He insisted on developing our own talent. That was the baseball way. He insisted that we put a competitive team on the field. He refused to charge major league ticket prices for minor leaguers."

Fetzer kept abreast on every player within the system, as he did with all matters pertaining to the club. He did so through daily telephone calls from Campbell and weekly written reports filed by each of his department heads. The reports summarized the status of each department. After scrutiny from Campbell, they were forwarded to Fetzer.

"This was a process that had been initiated with Mr. Fetzer's broadcast holdings," explained Carl Lee, long-time Fetzer confidant and chief of his broadcast holdings.

"Years ago, the FCC (Federal Communications Commission) frowned upon absentee ownership. Mr. Fetzer devised this system whereby he could be kept abreast of all his holdings through this series of communications. I would forward them to him for his perusal. He would return them with appropriate comments and suggestions. It was a way in which he could always remain current."

Because of baseball's daily volatility, Fetzer demanded more than weekly reports. Rarely did a day pass when Campbell didn't place at least one call to the boss.

Fetzer's demand for orderliness lent to a distinct delegation of power. Fetzer entrusted most of the baseball decisions to the professionals. He made his mark on other major matters.

"I set up a chain of command and found the most talented person I could to run each section or department," Fetzer explained. "Everyone in a particular section had a superior to whom to report on up the ladder. I allowed each department head a great deal of autonomy and allowed each the leeway to think through a problem. I didn't allow any department head to come to me and say here's a problem. He came to me with a recommendation. I might not agree with that recommendation, but then we worked out some sort of solution. That's the way we operated in all the years I owned the club."

Fetzer's method was designed to keep space between himself and his personnel. Employees were granted considerable latitude to resolve almost any situation.

"I wanted to maintain a fan's objectivity, or a fan's bias, for that matter," Fetzer explained. "If I let myself get too close to someone, I might set up a conflict of interest within my own mind."

Club officials were never hindered by Fetzer's interference. They addressed all problems through immediate supervisors.

"That's the John Fetzer school of baseball," Fetzer explained. "That's not to say I didn't care or that I was not always totally aware of what was going on. My system of weekly reports and regular phone calls kept me informed. I put a baseball man (Campbell) in charge and he ran the ship. I guess you could call that designed anonymity."

Throughout Fetzer's ownership, the Tigers were well known for their stability of front office personnel. While regular employee turnover in baseball has always been an accepted part of the game, most Tiger executives remained with the organization until retirement.

"You want to know Mr. Fetzer's secret?" offered Jack Tighe. Tighe was Fetzer's first manager in 1957 and worked for the organization for 54 years. "It was loyalty, plain and simple.

"There was an old sportscaster at Mr. Fetzer's station by the name of Hugh Harper. Right after Mr. Fetzer bought the team I remember Harper telling me: 'You'll never meet a guy like Mr. Fetzer.' That was it. He just left it hanging there and I didn't know at the time what he was talking about. I didn't know if I should be happy or go out looking for another job.

"Over the years I came to know what he meant. All you had to demonstrate to Mr. Fetzer was loyalty. And you'd get it back double. Mr. Fetzer truly liked and respected his employees. He was loyal to them and, in turn, they all were loyal to him. If that sounds too simple, then too bad, because that's the way it was."

Campbell set a major league record for number of years either as general manager, president or chairman. He filled one of those roles from 1962 until his discharge just before Mike Ilitch purchased the club in 1992. He originally joined the organization in 1949. Alice Sloane, executive secretary for baseball, worked for the club for forty-seven years until she was discharged in January, 1994, under the Ilitch ownership.

Tighe may hold the record for the most years served with one major league team. He signed with the Tigers as a minor league player in 1935. Except for a four-year stint with the Milwaukee Braves, he worked his entire professional career for the Tigers in a variety of baseball capacities. That covered a span of 54 years. His contract as a part-time scout was discontinued a year after the Ilitch purchase. There was a significant number of others who spent most of their professional careers with the Tigers.

"Baseball is a funny game," Tighe explained. "You look around at a lot of clubs and after a few years, guys get let go, and a lot of times for no apparent good reason. I'm talking about good, qualified baseball men. That's the nature of the game. You come to accept it.

"Fetzer never operated that way. If you were doing your job and you were a good person, you never felt like you were going to get fired. He didn't believe in that. He didn't believe in playing games with people's lives just because it was baseball. But he expected you to do your job and do it well."

Like so many of his employees, Fetzer preferred working behind the scenes. He never felt the need to flash his power with
public performances.

"He didn't need to do all that crap like some owners do,"
Tighe said. "He always preferred to work anonymously. And he
was always in control.

"He was like that right from the start. I remember when I
was named the Tiger manager in 1957. It was January and I was
home in Spring Lake (Michigan). I was supposed to give a speech
in Battle Creek and we got socked with a giant snowstorm. I couldn't
even get my car out of the garage.

"I called Carl Lee at the TV station. I told him:'Carl, I know Mr.
Fetzer wants me to make this speech, but I can't even make it down
my driveway.'

"It couldn't have been an hour later that a state highway truck
showed up at my house. He plowed the driveway and made sure I
could make it to the highway. I gave that speech and it was a
helluva good one.

"No one ever told me anything, but I know it was Mr. Fetzer
who arranged to get that truck there. It was just a little thing. But
that's the way he did everything."

Although viewed by many as being conservative and gray,
behind the scenes, Fetzer was one of the most innovative owners
of the modern game.

"People just never understood John Fetzer," said Milwaukee
Brewers Owner and Acting Baseball Commissioner Bud Selig. "He
was one of the most imaginative men I've ever met in my life. Next
to my father, he's the man I respect the most."

Fetzer was painfully aware of refinements in the game that
were crying to be made. He did not believe in change for the sake
of change alone. And he would never dare to tinker with the underlying essence of the game. However, he was a proponent of
revolution for matters he felt would enhance baseball's appeal.

In 1965, for instance, in a personal letter to *The Sporting News*,
Fetzer suggested some interesting proposals for baseball to consider.

"A critical examination of the length of the season is a necessity," he wrote. "Varied problems confronting ball clubs in the northern part of the United States, and who fight weather conditions
unheard of by other teams, make the scheduling problem and the
number of games to be played a tough nut to crack.

"There was a time in the history of our country when suspense could be held for six long months in order to find the outcome of an event. In this fast-moving age, where there is desperate competition for people's time every minute of the day, baseball will and must realize that changes are inevitable. We are trying to draw attention of fans away from radio, movies, television, the theater, travel, golf, boating, super highways, and numerous other leisure-time activities—even air conditioning. Many of these activities didn't exist when the players were transported to the ballpark in buckboards.

"...There is a woeful need to bring into being climactic events during the course of the season in order to sustain fan interest. Such ideas as inter-divisional, inter-league play or the team-of-the-month innovation should be carefully examined."

Because of added national television exposure that allowed fans to watch all players from both leagues, he later withdrew his support of inter-league play.

Fetzer did believe, however, there was a solution for the problem of diluted talent caused by expansion. He suggested that an experimental free substitution rule be tried. Under this rule, a player could return to the game three innings after having been removed. This would allow teams to cut their active rosters from 25 to 22 players. Three from each team then would be available for expansion franchises.

One of the first changes Fetzer initiated after buying the Tigers was to schedule more night games. Because Detroit always has been primarily a blue-collar town, he believed night games would provide more opportunities for the working man to see the Tigers.

Fetzer extended that philosophy with his approach toward television and baseball. Contrary to the convictions of many baseball traditionalists, Fetzer was convinced that expanded television coverage was good for the long-range health of the game. He believed that more exposure would entice rather than curtail fans from visiting the park. Consequently, he arranged for more local broadcasts. And, of course, he was instrumental in developing national telecasts, which now offer some sort of game almost each night of the week.

Fetzer, without question, established a business-like environment after taking control of the Tigers. As with any successful business venture, Fetzer initiated budgets for the various departments.

Most of the profits that were generated by the club were pumped into the minor league system from which Fetzer was determined the Tigers would develop most of their players.

It was a simple philosophy for a simple game. Fetzer loved the beauty of both. It provided a reassuring comfort for Tiger fans for almost three decades.

CHAPTER 11

The Big Eye and Big Smiles

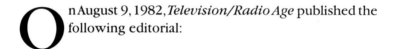

O n August 9, 1982, *Television/Radio Age* published the following editorial:

Last week the Baseball Hall of Fame at Cooperstown, N.Y., inducted three baseball heroes—Hank Aaron, Frank Robinson, Travis Jackson, plus A.B. Happy Chandler. Chandler had succeeded Judge Kenesaw Mountain Landis as commissioner in 1945 and was dismissed five years later by the baseball owners. It was an imposing group, but the man that should be enshrined in the Baseball Hall of Fame is John E. Fetzer, owner of the Detroit Tigers. Fetzer is a widely respected broadcaster who owns WKZO-TV Kalamazoo and other broadcast properties in midwest markets.

Fetzer has already been recognized by his peers in the broadcast industry. He received the Distinguished Service Award given by the National Association of Broadcasters at the convention in 1969. In October, 1965, he put together on behalf of Major League Baseball a plan to package the 'Game of the Week' on an expanded basis and the World Series for a rights figure of $50 million. Up to that point the 'Game of the Week' had been blacked out in all major league cities. It seemed like an insurmountable task to get the baseball moguls to agree to allow the 'Game of the Week' to

come into their local areas. The only restriction on Fetzer's plan
was that the games would be blacked out in the home markets of
the teams playing."

In spite of its overwhelming influence on modern society,
even the television industry lacks the power to nominate membership for Baseball's Hall of Fame.

Nevertheless, the premise for Fetzer's enshrinement goes
beyond television suggestion. The patient wisdom of history perhaps one day will guarantee Fetzer's proper place in Cooperstown.
If so, Fetzer's imaginative and revolutionary accomplishment of unit-
ing all baseball owners under a shared national television contract
will serve as the defining standard.

Modern fans have become spoiled by television's nightly, full
menu of major league games. With a remote in one hand and a
beverage in the other, fans all over the country can flip through a
variety of telecasts. It may not be like sitting in the park, but it's a
whole lot more convenient. An evening without this panorama of
scheduling now seems impossible to comprehend. Of course, there
will be a few games from which to choose; if a fans gets bored with
one game, they can simply switch to another game in the other
league.

But it took a revolutionary approach in baseball's television
philosophy to get the game as much exposure as we take for granted
today.

The concept of each franchise sharing equally in the staggering figures of television revenues is now the accepted norm. Franchises would find it difficult to operate without those revenues.
Even the public seems to have become accustomed to the almost
obscene dollar amounts that each telecast generates.

Thirty years ago, however, that certainly wasn't the case. And
if it wasn't for the revolutionary television package created by Fetzer,
national baseball telecasts wouldn't be only a click of the remote
away.

"Absolutely, there's no question that John's original television
contract was the forerunner of today's package," said former Baseball Commissioner Bowie Kuhn.

Of course, revenues from baseball's current national television rights dwarf those of even five years ago. Baseball, in fact, now
bases its economic foundation on TV income. Teams now have

turned their attention to the construction of new stadiums with huge revenue-generating luxury suites.

That old reliable money-making television package, however, remains the gold mine of all sports. If the big eye ever decided to pull the plug on its coverage, the lights in every ball park wouldn't go dark, but they certainly wouldn't shine as brightly as they do now.

The revenues derived from Fetzer's original package were staggering for their time. And it was that package from which today's big bucks bonanza evolved.

"There's no question Mr. Fetzer led the way," said former American League President Lee MacPhail. At the time of the original contract, MacPhail served as general manager of the Baltimore Orioles.

"Any doubts and concerns that the owners had about that package, he was able to dispel. A lot of owners were reluctant to surrender their individual broadcast rights. It was primarily the respect that the owners felt for John that convinced them to go along with the idea. It's possible that without this package, baseball wouldn't enjoy today's lucrative rights fees."

Fetzer's concept of each club sharing equally in the untapped resources of a national television network package was an obvious extension of his conviction to unity of spirit, particularly in an industry such as baseball, where the strength of the whole is measured by the power of its individual parts.

"Baseball is a little different than other businesses in our economy," explained former Tiger boss Jim Campbell.

"It's all right for one supermarket to swallow up all the mom and pop corner stores. That's good business. It's the way things work in a free-market economy.

"But it's bad business in baseball when any franchise is struggling. In baseball, everybody needs everybody else. What good does it do, for instance, for the Yankees to drive the Brewers out of business? Nothing. It hurts New York as much as it does Milwaukee."

At the time of Fetzer's revolutionary vision for television, clubs depended primarily on game attendance for financial stability. And in those years, there were several struggling franchises.

Without even the now modest sum from that national TV contract of those early days, a few clubs would have been in a fight for their very survival.

Fetzer was named to chair the Major League Baseball Television Committee in 1963, one year after taking sole ownership of the Tigers. He was a logical choice for the owners. Fetzer had made a fortune in building, purchasing, operating and selling various broadcast holdings across the country.

"The owners knew that Mr. Fetzer understood the industry," said long-time confidant Carl Lee, who headed Fetzer's broadcast empire. "He was there in the business right from the start. He defined the industry. He had pioneered so many of its elements. He knew the language. He knew all the powerful people."

And even more important for baseball, he knew what the television industry could mean to the game.

To suggest that major league baseball would have gone out of business without such a contract overstates its significance. To understate its import, however, is equally naive, especially in light of television's current billion-dollar investment that encompasses networks, ESPN, local over-the-air broadcasts and countless local, regional and national cable productions.

Fetzer didn't single-handedly direct the sophistication of what has evolved into a spectacular studio sport, but he certainly laid the foundation.

For those pioneer efforts when few were blessed with the vision of where this marriage between baseball and television may lead, it seems perfectly appropriate to consider Fetzer for Hall of Fame status.

"There's no question that without Mr. Fetzer's efforts, a few for sale signs would have cropped up around both leagues," Campbell said.

"Once he really got involved with baseball, he always looked out for the good of the game. At times it might have cost the Tigers some money for the moment. But in the long run, he knew that if something was good for the game, then eventually it was good for every team.

"Without a doubt, Mr. Fetzer brought ownership in baseball to its senses in regard to what could be done with television. The owners had been helter-skelter. Everybody had a little different deal and their own axes to grind. The big city markets dominated. Mr. Fetzer eventually prevailed on all of them to use common sense, to group together, to act as one rather than a gaggle of individuals. That TV contract was the savior of baseball, in my opinion.

"A lot of people in baseball agreed in principal to what Mr. Fetzer wanted to do, but they also thought there was no way in hell it could ever be accomplished. Well, he did it. To me, that was Mr. Fetzer's greatest contribution to our game."

Kuhn concurs with Campbell's speculation.

"What you have to keep in mind is that John delivered this magnificent package with NBC," Kuhn explained. "And John was a CBS man. The number-one television station that he owned was a CBS affiliate. The relationship between baseball and NBC was one of the first really rich ones that I had ever encountered."

When Fetzer assumed the chair of baseball's television committee, there was no national contract. Most clubs relied upon the sale of their local packages to generate the major portion of their television revenues.

Prior to Fetzer's deal, there was only a modified network game-of-the-week package that was limited to select teams. In 1962, major league games were televised on Saturdays and Sundays under individual contracts with CBS and NBC. The Yankees, Orioles, Cubs, Cardinals and Phillies shared about one million dollars from CBS. The Tigers, White Sox, Indians, Twins, Reds, Braves and Pirates split $700,000 from NBC. The other teams received nothing. Only the home teams received revenues with the visitors serving as non-paid "straight men."

In 1963, the networks paid $2.2 million for major league baseball with the Yankees getting the lion's share. The Yankees hosted 22 dates at $25,000 a game, for a total of $550,000.

To their credit, and perhaps because of CBS's ownership of the franchise, the Yankees endorsed the Fetzer plan.

"It had become apparent to me that this piecemeal operation was giving the buyer all the advantage," Fetzer said. "It simply was the old case of divide and rule."

Commissioner Ford Frick recognized the merits of Fetzer's initiative. He sent a directive to all clubs urging that none make any network deal before consulting with Fetzer.

"We will never have a sound program unless selfishness and individual promotion is tossed out the window and a program established on an overall basis," Frick wrote.

Fetzer's plan called for equal revenue sharing among all clubs; even those whose games were not chosen to be televised benefitted.

Through his efforts and the backing of the commissioner's office, Fetzer negotiated a deal that guaranteed $300,000 per club for the 1965 season. It rose to $325,000 in 1966. Currently, the revenues received from television rights by individual clubs rival those generated by some teams' paid admissions.

Fetzer needed the cooperation of the commissioner's office in order to make his concept work. He convinced the commissioner and the rest of the owners that the broadcast rights to the World Series and All-Star Game must be part of the package.

"It is always necessary to negotiate from strength rather than weakness," Fetzer explained. "We soon learned we were negotiating from weakness when we were attempting to sell the game-of-the-week as a separate package."

With baseball including its prize jewels as part of a complete package, it presented a "take it or leave it" premise for the networks to consider.

All three networks were interested in the proposal and bidding became brisk. NBC was the first winner, landing the initial contract. Since then, the television industry has continued to explode, raising the revenues realized by baseball today to unbelievable amounts.

Success with this critical segment of the industry thrust Fetzer squarely into a position of untouchable influence that lasted throughout his baseball career.

Fetzer pushed boldly to stretch baseball's boundaries with television further than anyone imagined. Although it achieved only fragmentary success, his dream for a network prime-time Monday Night Baseball Spectacular never quite developed into the image he had envisioned.

This ambitious vision, however, may have planted the seed for what has become an American sports television institution— Monday Night Football.

"It's a legitimate speculation," Kuhn said.

It was September 25, 1963, when Fetzer first proposed a baseball Monday Night Game of the Week to CBS Vice President William MacPhail in a confidential letter.

Fetzer proposed that CBS carry 26 Monday night baseball "extravaganzas" in prime time. The program, of course, would center around a featured game. The rest of the three-hour slot would be filled with "live and taped interviews with big-time baseball stars, celebrities that are baseball fans, kid baseball features showing the training programs in baseball camps, etc." The length of the average game in those days rarely went past two-and-a-half hours.

Fetzer's proposal called for the program to run from 8 to 11 p.m., Eastern Time, with no blackout areas, to attract powerful national advertisers.

Convinced it would work, Fetzer devoted an inordinate amount of time trying to make this innovative concept come to life. He estimated that his Monday night plan would produce a million dollars for each team. More importantly, it would thrust baseball into the forefront of another level of exposure.

For a variety of reasons, however, the concept never really got rolling. CBS didn't want to tinker with its powerful Monday night lineup of shows, even if it was only for a few weeks of the television season. NBC was booked with the political conventions and the summer Olympics. ABC was skeptical about having enough viewer interest.

Certainly, the National Football League got the message. Together with ABC, it has refined the Monday night concept into a gold mine.

"We tried a limited amount of network Monday night games in the early '70s," Kuhn said. "But baseball is harder to sell numbers on a national network than football. Baseball is much more local than football. Football performs much differently to a national network than does baseball."

Unlike many baseball traditionalists who feared that too much television exposure would dilute fan interest and keep people from going to the park, Fetzer believed an increased amount would help to bolster attendance.

An October 1, 1973, editorial in *Broadcasting* magazine paid tribute to Fetzer's vision:

> For the past decade, thanks to the sagacity of broadcaster-baseball club owner John E. Fetzer, major league games have been telecast at least once a week nationally, while most out-of-town games and some home contests have been broadcast locally or through regional networks.

> The lesson should be obvious. It was initially radio and later radio plus television that stimulated ballpark attendance, attracting new fans, including women and adolescents. Football clubs know only too well that without radio and subsequent TV exposure the sport would have continued largely in amateur collegiate confines.

Consider the onset of the current professional sports explosion. The entrepreneurs owe most to the broadcast media. The baseball success this year was achieved not because of but in spite of the blackouts.

Mr. Fetzer, chairman of the Fetzer station group and owner of the Detroit Tigers, has proved a prophet with honor. He stimulated the Monday night network spectaculars against tough odds. It is a lesson that Pete Rozelle, the pro football commissioner, and his club owners should rehearse.

Not only did owners reap benefits from baseball's expanded television coverage but also the players. Because of these increased sources of revenues, players' salaries began their limitless upward spiral.

C.C. Johnson Spink, publisher of *The Sporting News,* wrote to Fetzer after baseball had signed its first contract with NBC: "I don't know how many notes of appreciation you will get from the ballplayers, but every one of them ought to sit down and write a thank you note to you."

Fetzer's concern for proper baseball exposure was not restricted to the major leagues. He also felt that baseball would benefit from the promotion of top minor league games. In the late '60s, Fetzer proposed a national telecast of a Triple-A game for each Sunday afternoon.

"The greatest need in baseball today is a bold new plan to build a sound economic base under minor league baseball and, at the same time, create a sufficient pool of talent to bring ultimate expansion to the major leagues," Fetzer wrote. "The increased cost in running minor league baseball, most of which falls to the major league working agreements, plus fewer teams and lower attendance, indicates that some new economic base for the minors must be established.

"At least one solution to the problem would be a new approach to the minor league television relationship. Just as a half-dozen years ago we started to talk about a sound plan for major league baseball in its relation to television, we now suggest a sweeping new plan for Class AAA baseball.

"A Class AAA coast-to-coast baseball game could be established each Sunday afternoon throughout the summer to be seen in practically every television market, including major league cities, with minimal restrictions."

Maybe it was too progressive. Maybe it ran far too much ahead of its time. For a variety of reasons, however, including the budding of numerous other professional sports, the idea never materialized. But its lack of fulfillment never deterred Fetzer's imaginative approach toward broadening baseball's boundaries.

Certainly, the fruits of that imagination were appreciated by his peers. Without the benefits derived from the national television contract, for instance, some of his fellow owners may have been forced from the game.

A letter dated August 10, 1967, from Charles O. Finley to Fetzer, signified the importance of the unified national television contract. At the time, Finley owned the Kansas City Royals before moving the franchise to Oakland. He wrote the following:

> I just had to take the time to express my sincere thanks and appreciation to you and the Television Committee for the success you accomplished on behalf of we owners in baseball. Needless to say, our contract with NBC has been my salvation in staying in the game I love so much. Again, my sincere thanks and appreciation.

Chicago Cubs' owner Phil Wrigley perhaps didn't need the financial boost as much as Finley. But having been in the game for as long as he had, he marveled at Fetzer's accomplishment. In a congratulatory letter to Fetzer, he expressed the game's unified sense of gratitude:

> This letter is being written principally to again express my admiration for the marvelous job you did in getting all the members of both leagues and the Commissioner's office together so that for the first time we could put up a united front, and having been around professional baseball for some 40 years, I know that was not easy because of the competition between the two leagues on the field, and the competition between the individual clubs of each league on the field. In fact, I even told a Congressional hearing some years back that the reason I referred to professional baseball always instead of organized baseball was because I thought it was less organized than anything I had ever been connected with, but in one case at least you have proven me wrong, as you have succeeded in getting us organized as far as our broadcasting is concerned which I was beginning to believe would be impossible.

John McHale, then president of the Milwaukee Braves, echoed those sentiments. He wrote to Fetzer:

> The entire Braves organization joins me in thanking you for the tremendous job you have done in putting together the program for the television Game of the Week. In my estimation it is one of the greatest steps that 'unified baseball' has taken in my time in the game.
>
> I happen to know how much time and energy you have given to this project. I also am aware of the tremendous roadblocks you personally had to overcome within and outside baseball to accomplish this great goal. To me, the success of this has been due to the efforts of one man—John Fetzer.

Now, more than three decades since its inception, baseball's marriage with national television seems to be insoluble. The revenues now realized from the broadcast rights at one time seemed utterly inconceivable.

Is the game better for it? That's a question for baseball historians and network executives to determine. The mere fact that baseball today shares in such riches can be traced to the imagination of John E. Fetzer.

And from that spark of genius, Fetzer forged a mountain of change that will continue to re-shape the game for decades to come.

CHAPTER 12

The Most Powerful Force

In 1975, at baseball's winter convention, Bill Veeck staged a comeback to the game as a part owner and managing partner of the Chicago White Sox.

At the time, Veeck's appeal to several owners ranked slightly higher than that of player labor leader Marvin Miller's. Veeck was the carnival barker turned baseball executive. He brought to baseball the wonder of the exploding scoreboard. For Veeck, no gadget or gimmick seemed too outrageous. He was the one-legged huckster who believed the only purpose for a necktie was to protect a shirt from spilled soup. That, of course, didn't make him all bad.

For a variety of reasons, mostly involving a conflict of philosophy with several owners, most American League voters vowed to deny the approval of Veeck's purchase attempt. They had concocted an array of roadblocks to stymie his return. One of the principal hindrances was a complicated system of meeting financial approval.

Veeck was stalled, but his motor never quit running. He parried each restriction with a corresponding solution. Nevertheless, his rapscallion personality prickled enough owners to keep them unified in their effort to deny his return to the game until John Fetzer took the floor to speak in the closed door meeting.

"It was quite classic in the way John Fetzer operated," recalled then American League President Lee MacPhail, who was actually satisfied that Veeck had satisfied all of the restrictions placed upon him.

"John remained quiet during most of the discussion. That was usually the manner in which he conducted himself. Toward the end of the meeting, he stood up and endorsed Veeck's proposal. It was short. I don't recall exactly what he said. I think it was more the fact that it was John himself who was speaking and the other owners had so much respect for him. At any rate, they took another vote and Veeck was approved."

Fetzer was never particularly fond of Veeck. He had, after all, made an unsuccessful bid to buy the Tigers in 1956. Afterward, Veeck charged Fetzer and his syndicate with submitting an improper bid and publicly castigated the group, but Fetzer felt compelled to do the honorable thing, so he placed all personal feelings aside.

"It's true the man (Veeck) had called me a son of a bitch after I had purchased the Tigers fair and square," Fetzer explained, "but what's right is right. The man had met all the conditions we had set forth. There was no alternative but to do the right thing."

The "right thing" would not have been done, however, if not for the influence of Fetzer. Once the announcement of the sale was made, the story of Fetzer's persuasive speech quickly leaked to the press.

"He doesn't say much and, by design, he stands in the background," wrote veteran *Chicago Tribune* sports writer Jerome Holtzman, "but there's no question that John Fetzer is the most powerful force in baseball."

So thanks to the man who had prevented his return to major league ownership almost two decades prior, Veeck was back. Despite his conflicting philosophy with Fetzer, eventually even Veeck conceded the power of the Tiger owner. In 1979, long-time Dodger Owner Walter O'Malley died. Similar to Fetzer in the American League, it was O'Malley who, behind the scenes, pulled the strings of the National League.

"George Steinbrenner (Yankee owner) would like to be the new O'Malley, but I don't think he can do it," Veeck was quoted. "The strong man in the American League is John Fetzer. He's very intelligent, very balanced, very thoughtful. And he's as wealthy as any. He's a man of substance. He could influence me more than all the rest because he makes sense."

The extent of Fetzer's power in baseball was measured more meaningfully by the way he chose to use it rather than its mere amount.

"Because he was such a private person, a lot of people never realized how powerful he was in baseball," said Hall of Famer and former Tiger George Kell.

"I bet half the people in Michigan never knew who owned the Tigers when he did. That's the way he wanted it. It was by design. He never flaunted that power. He never flaunted his money. He never flaunted anything. He didn't have to. He was the man in control."

That power spread far beyond Michigan and the Tigers. It touched every aspect of the game.

"The owners recognized that he was always looking out for the good of the game and not just the selfish interests of the Tigers," MacPhail said.

"His power was felt in both leagues, particularly the American. There was Mr. Fetzer in the American League and Walter O'Malley in the National. Whatever these two recommended, the other owners would pretty much follow. They were that well respected."

Needless to say, Fetzer's vision of the game was not necessarily the path that owners always chose to follow, particularly toward the end of Fetzer's career when the make-up of ownership shifted from sportsmen to arms of giant corporations.

For the majority of his career, however, Fetzer devoted much of his time serving on a variety of decision-making committees and counseling a number of fellow owners on day-to-day matters that arose in franchises of both leagues.

"There is no question that for the greater part of Mr. Fetzer's ownership he was the power behind the throne," Kell said. "It didn't matter if he was on a particular committee or not. If there was a major decision to be made and baseball was concerned about it, all the owners would call him to find out firsthand what he thought about the matter. Whichever way he viewed an issue usually sealed the deal."

The baseball power Fetzer enjoyed was something for which he had not campaigned. Power of that stature is earned, not acquired by political strategy. Owners, commissioners and league presidents relied upon his insight. The trust he generated among his peers never was betrayed.

Fetzer handled his far-reaching influence gracefully and nearly anonymously.

"He loved the game dearly and was concerned about its future," MacPhail explained. "Even when he tried to remove himself from certain committees, we always convinced him that he had to stay."

Fetzer firmly believed that the health of the game is measured solely by the combined strength of all of its franchises. He was convinced that baseball could only be strong through the unity of spirit of all franchise owners.

"You know there are two kinds of owners," said former Baseball Commissioner Bowie Kuhn. "One always wants to know 'How does it affect my club?' Then there are those who think first of how it affects the game. Emphatically, John belonged at the top of the latter group. He was always looking out for the best interests of baseball. A man of considerable wealth, a religious man with a fine ethical sense, who always sought the good course; John didn't struggle with himself.

"I always considered John and Walter O'Malley as the elder statesmen of their leagues. They were among the most revered and most respected men in baseball. They were very different in personality, yet very similar in their dedication to the game. Because of John's approach of quiet, reasoned persuasion that seemed bland in contrast to the flamboyance of some other owners, he was wrongly pegged as a stand-pat conservative in baseball matters. All along, he was one of the strongest and most responsible supporters of innovation in the game."

Fetzer's power was established from serving as chair of the Major League Baseball Television Committee from 1963-1971. Through his success in this critical area, he went on to serve on a variety of other powerful committees, including the prestigious Executive Council.

"The owners relied heavily on him to come up with an acceptable television contract," MacPhail said. "They all knew how successful he had been in the broadcast industry. There were several who were somewhat reluctant to relinquish their individual rights. But John convinced them it was for the good of all. And certainly history has proven he couldn't have been more correct."

Fetzer's expertise was not limited solely to broadcasting.

"He was such an intelligent man," Kell recalled. "At times when I was talking with him, I almost felt afraid. Not because of the way he acted, but because he was so intelligent he almost seemed to know what you were thinking.

"There was nothing frivolous about him. There was no small talk. He was all business at all times. Yet he was so concerned. He knew how to listen. That's a tremendous gift.

"He was a very reticent man. He was a quiet leader. When he spoke, the other owners listened."

In 1981, Fetzer was bestowed with a host of honors. He was the recipient of the August A. Busch Jr. Award for meritorious service to baseball. The John E. Fetzer Award for meritorious service to baseball was established in his name and he was the first recipient. Neither of these awards are presented annually. They are given rarely and only to persons of the game's highest order. He also was elected Honorary Vice President of the American League.

Certainly Fetzer appreciated such prestigious awards, but his greatest satisfaction was derived from his contributions to the game.

As Fetzer gave the nod to approve Veeck in 1975, he shook his head the other way seven years later to block wealthy land developer Edward DeBartolo in his attempt to purchase the White Sox. In addition to various real estate holdings around the country, DeBartolo also was the owner of three horse racing tracks.

Commissioner Kuhn had come out publicly with a strong sentiment against gambling interests of any kind for anyone involved with baseball.

"Not that there hadn't been race tracks involved with baseball before," Kuhn explained. "John Galbreath (Pittsburgh Pirates owner) had an interest in Churchill Downs. But I was increasingly concerned about the gambling issue. I felt we had to distance ourselves from the gambling as much as possible. So at a certain point, I said no more race tracks. We could grandfather in what we had, but we had to stop there.

"There was some back and forth within baseball of whether we needed to be that rigid. But then he (DeBartolo) did a very foolish thing. Because I was dragging my feet on the matter, he had a guy who ran his New Orleans race track who publicly accused me of being anti-Italian. That was really laughable. That really turned the tide against him."

It certainly did with Fetzer. In fact, it may have destroyed a secret plan that Fetzer had devised to help get DeBartolo approved.

Fetzer had created a system by which DeBartolo could divest himself of his horse racing interests and therefore be cleared for American League approval. MacPhail had arranged for a private meeting between Fetzer and DeBartolo the evening before the final vote was to be taken. It was at that meeting that Fetzer shared his solution.

From the day he helped place Bowie Kuhn in office, Fetzer had been a staunch supporter, as well as a strong personal friend, of the commissioner. The ill-spoken remark about Kuhn ended the campaign Fetzer was structuring on DeBartolo's behalf. At the next day's meeting, Fetzer withdrew his support of DeBartolo, and with it went any chance for the would-be owner to acquire the White Sox.

Fetzer had been instrumental in helping to get Kuhn appointed Commissioner in 1969. Had the insult at Kuhn not been leveled, Fetzer may have swung the owners into welcoming DeBartolo into their exclusive club.

Fetzer's loyalty to friends and employees never wavered, even to those in the face of public ridicule. That certainly was the case with General William Eckert, who endured a rather forgettable term as Baseball Commissioner from 1965 to 1969. Fetzer had been significantly responsible for placing the retired Air Force general in the position. One of the problems that undermined Eckert's term of office, however, was that the owners never fully followed through with the restructuring of the game's hierarchy as had been recommended by Fetzer and Pittsburgh Pirates owner John Galbreath.

Because of Fetzer's brilliance in creating the network television package for baseball and his overall business acumen, he was picked to play a pivotal role in the selection of a new commissioner. Ford Frick was retiring from the position after the 1965 season after 14 years of service.

The office of baseball commissioner was created in 1920. It was born out of the 1919 scandal in which several players of the Chicago White Sox were charged with throwing games to the Cincinnati Reds for gambling purposes. The integrity of baseball had been shaken to its foundation. The position of commissioner was created to help restore the game's image, keep it honest and maintain public confidence.

Judge Kenesaw Mountain Landis, the man the owners selected for this most sensitive position, was a man of unimpeachable integrity. He ruled the game with an iron fist. He was provided with almost limitless power for the next 24 years.

In the time between his departure and Frick's retirement, however, the internal workings of the game had undergone some radical changes. Part of that metamorphosis reflected America's shifting attitude toward liberalism and use of the legal system. The commissioner's position was stripped of its wide-sweeping powers when owners changed baseball's bylaws in two critical areas.

First, a paragraph that had prevented club owners from taking grievances to court was eliminated. Therefore, if an owner disputed the commissioner's decision on a matter, he was free to take his case to court. Secondly, a clause was added stating that no one act or procedure agreed upon by the owners could be construed as being detrimental to baseball.

"Whether intentional or not," Frick told the owners at the time of his departure, "this clause definitely limited the authority of the commissioner to act positively in such present operational problems as expansion, transfer of franchises, handling of television and radio problems, and denied his authority to penalize or stop, as detrimental to baseball, any action taken by any league or club in compliance with joint-action rules."

Frick also delivered a parting message to the owners that very much reflected the views that Fetzer had promoted since his arrival in the sport.

"So long as the owners and operators refuse to look beyond the day and the hour ... so long as clubs and individuals persist in gaining personal headlines through public criticism of their associates ... so long as baseball people are unwilling to abide by the rules which they themselves make ... so long as they are willing to sacrifice the welfare of the whole for the benefit of the individual ... and so long as expediency is permitted to replace sound judgment, there can be no satisfactory solution," Frick said. "Baseball people must face up to these problems, must settle upon a sound and satisfactory policy, and must then unite in seeing that policy through to successful conclusion."

Nevertheless, the game was changing. And so had the position of commissioner to comply with the restrictions of its new definition.

In late March of 1965, Fetzer and Galbreath were selected as co-chairmen of a two-person committee to screen candidates for the commissioner's position.

The committee received 156 nominees and was charged with screening and then submitting about 50 candidates to the 20 owners. Fetzer submitted no candidate. But he strongly suggested that the commissioner's office demanded complete restructuring.

"At the time, I thought that one man could not handle the job himself," Fetzer said. "It was too monstrous a task. I preferred a tandem replacement. I wanted my fellow owners to do lots of legwork in checking out the credentials of prospects in their areas. Some of them did, but most of them didn't."

Fetzer envisioned an office whereby a deputy commissioner would be appointed to handle all baseball matters of both leagues. Each league would serve somewhat as a division under a parent corporation. The commissioner would hold overall power and serve as a representative of the highest ethics the game had to offer.

But the process seemed to be mired in quicksand. Neither Fetzer nor Galbreath could manage to get the body of owners to agree upon a selection or even make meaningful suggestions. Later in the summer, the screening committee added the Cubs' Phil Wrigley and the Angels' Bob Reynolds.

The owners announced that the commissioner's office would include an administrator, a director of player affairs, a director of public information, a director of broadcasting and a director of amateur baseball.

Owners, however, still could not agree upon who the new head man would be. At the winter convention in Miami, before the national media could ridicule baseball even more for its inability to name a new commissioner, the screening committee unanimously endorsed Eckert. He was approved, along with Lee MacPhail who would leave his position with the Orioles to serve as the baseball administrator.

While Eckert was a three-star general who had served admirably in the private sector of industry after his retirement from the Air Force, he never became acclimated to the world of baseball. His administration became the subject of ridicule by the media. After three inglorious seasons, he removed himself from the position. Neither Eckert nor the hastily contrived administrative staff could function with efficiency.

Fetzer accepted his responsibility for appointing Eckert to the post. He remained convinced, however, that under better circumstances and proper preparation, the organizational approach to the commissioner's office was necessary for the overall health of the game.

With Eckert's resignation, baseball again found itself in the embarrassing situation of functioning without a head. And once again, bickering between American and National League owners resembled a joint convention of Democrats and Republicans.

Fetzer persuaded his colleagues that a new commissioner must be announced immediately to avoid further embarrassment from the media and general fandom.

Although he came into the game with perhaps a shade more National League experience, Bowie Kuhn was named interim commissioner for one year in December, 1968, at baseball's winter convention. Kuhn was a 42-year-old Princeton alumnus and graduate of the University of Virginia Law School. He had been a member of the New York law firm of Wilkie, Farr & Gallagher, which had represented the National League since 1936.

"I was sitting in my room with Sandy Hadden, an attorney for the American League," Kuhn recalled, "when I got a call to come up to Walter O'Malley's suite. John Fetzer of the Tigers and Bob Reynolds of the Angels were there. I was stunned when they asked if I would serve as interim commissioner for a year to help work out the restructuring of the administration of baseball."

Kuhn, of course, accepted. The term "interim" was dropped from his title within the year, and he served the position until stepping down after the 1984 season.

It didn't matter that Kuhn had a National League background. Fetzer was particularly impressed with Kuhn's ethical approach to the game.

"I think John and I shared the same ideals," Kuhn said. "He placed the game on a pedestal far above that of normal business concerns. For him, nothing mattered more than baseball always reflecting the highest standard of ethics.

"I felt the same way. Throughout my career as commissioner, I'd often play a little game when I'd get into a taxi cab. I'd ask the driver: 'Of all the professional sports, which is the most honest?' They'd always answer baseball. To me, that was the source of greatest satisfaction."

As concerned as Fetzer was with the overall condition of baseball, he was equally concerned with the status of his Tigers. Particularly when it came to matters of organization and human relations.

Although it is presumptuous to credit Fetzer for the desegregation of Lakeland, Florida, where the Tigers have conducted spring training since 1946 (with the exception of three years during World

War II), it is perfectly valid to suggest that his influence helped to speed the spread of integration in the central Florida city.

In the early '60s, at about the time Fetzer had taken control of the Tigers, race relations had become a sensitive issue throughout America and particularly the South. For spring training with the Tigers, black players were given the option of being placed in the homes of local black families or staying at the integrated Tigertown facilities.

A sentiment for total integration, however, was being sounded all over the country. Fetzer wanted to rectify the Tiger situation immediately. In 1962, he ordered Jim Campbell to make certain all players were treated completely equal regardless of their race.

Lakeland, of course, had been raised in the custom of separation of blacks and whites. It was not a tradition that would easily fade. The city, however, also was aware of Fetzer's love affair with the state of Arizona. It certainly did not wish to run the risk of losing the Tigers, which had become a source of significant tourist revenue during the winter months.

Without fanfare, Campbell initiated negotiations with the mayor, members of the city commission and the Lakeland Chamber of Commerce. The Tigers sought complete integration for their players regarding hotels and restaurants.

"All of these men have recognized this problem, not only with baseball, but in other enterprises," Campbell reported to Fetzer during his negotiations. "They feel that the time has come when they must take a stand."

Campbell reached an agreement with the Holiday Inn to house all major league players on a non-segregated basis starting with spring training of 1963. The hotel was located only four blocks from Henley Field, where the Tigers trained at the time.

"In a situation which could have become explosive, Campbell worked out an agreement which was completely satisfactory, with equal accommodations for all of our players—whether it be living quarters or eating facilities," Fetzer said.

It was another example of how Fetzer's influence permeated the game throughout his career.

"When you strip it down to basics, there were two simple reasons why John Fetzer enjoyed the power he did," Kell explained.

"First of all, the man was so intelligent. In all of his businesses, he had a vision of how things could be made to be better. He had a vision to improve things without turning them into a carnival. You must remember that this man had the opportunity to be an Ambassador for the United States under several administrations. But he had too many other things going to accept.

"Secondly, the man was honest. His word was his bond. You never needed a written contract when dealing with John Fetzer. All you needed was a handshake."

He left the imprint of that hand on the whole state of Michigan, the Tigers, and the game he loved.

The youngster who would eventually become one of baseball's most powerful owners is pictured here with his mother, Della (left) and his sister, Hattie (right). *(Photo courtesy of Fetzer Institute Archives)*

John Fetzer as a young boy, in Decatur, Indiana, about 1908. *(Photo courtesy of Fetzer Institute Archives)*

This publicity shot of Fetzer was taken in 1928 for WEMC Radio. He was that station's full-time chief engineer and part-time announcer. *(Photo courtesy of Fetzer Institute Archives)*

At the close of World War II, John Fetzer was part of a select group of broadcasters invited to Europe to assess the condition of the radio stations. During that trip the group met with General Dwight D. Eisenhower at Supreme Headquarters for the Expeditionary Force. Fetzer is seated to the left of the future president. *(Photo courtesy of U.S. Army Signal Corps)*

Fetzer (at the microphone) during the New Year's Day 1949 dedication of WKZO Radio's new "Block-Long Radio City" in Kalamazoo. *(Photo courtesy of WKZO, Fetzer Institute Archives)*

Fetzer (left) and Carl Lee, then chief engineer of Fetzer Broadcasting, at the transmitter for WKZO-TV during its inaugural broadcast in 1950. *(Photo courtesy of WKZO, Fetzer Institute Archives)*

John Fetzer traveled all over the world and met with numerous dignitaries, including the Shah of Iran, during a 1952 press and radio editors tour of Europe and the Middle East. *(Photo courtesy of Fetzer Institute Archives)*

Spike Briggs (front, second from left) signed over control of the Tigers to Fetzer's syndicate in 1956. *(Photo courtesy of Fetzer Institute Archives)*

John Fetzer (far right) is pictured at the "freedom bell", the symbol of the Crusade for Freedom in West Germany, in November, 1956, only months after his group was successful in purchasing the Detroit Tigers. A prominent group of American broadcast giants was asked to visit installations of Radio Free Europe and Free Europe Press. Pictured left to right are Kenyon Brown, Leonard Reinsch, Paul A. O'Bryan and Fetzer. Brown and O'Bryan were part of Fetzer's Tiger syndicate. *(Photo courtesy of Fetzer Institute Archives)*

Above all else, John Fetzer was the Tigers' No. 1 fan. Cheering at an opening day game with Fetzer were his wife, Rhea, Tiger executive vice president Harry Sisson and Mrs. Sisson (far left). *(Photo courtesy of* Detroit News)

Norm Cash was a particular favorite of Tiger fans. He captured the American League batting title in 1961. *(Photo by Thomas Donoghue)*

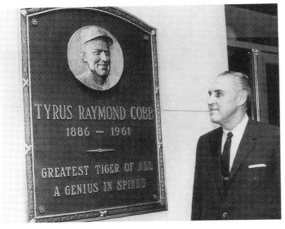

TYRUS RAYMOND COBB
1886 — 1961

GREATEST TIGER OF ALL
A GENIUS IN SPIKES

Fetzer at the 1963 dedication of a plaque honoring Ty Cobb, the greatest Tiger player of them all. *(Photo courtesy of Detroit Tigers)*

Two Tiger stars, Al Kaline (left) and George Kell (right), both received their start in baseball broadcasting from John Fetzer. *(Photo courtesy of Detroit Tigers)*

Fetzer quickly assumed a position of subtle leadership in baseball, often serving as behind-the-scenes counsel to Commissioner Bowie Kuhn (center) and American League President and Hall of Famer Joe Cronin (right). *(Photo courtesy of Detroit Tigers)*

Bill Freehan was one of the most knowledgeable Tiger catchers in the history of the franchise. Signed off the campus of the University of Michigan, Freehan became a perennial all-star. *(Photo courtesy of Detroit Tigers)*

Willie Horton slid safely across home plate as teammate Jim Northrup watched. Horton, signed off the Detroit sandlots, remains one of the most popular players ever to wear the Tiger uniform. *(Photo courtesy of Detroit Tigers)*

Gates Brown was the deadliest pinch hitter in Tiger history. The Gator always performed best when the game was on the line. *(Photo courtesy of Detroit Tigers)*

Mickey Lolich was the perfect workingman's pitcher in a workingman's town. He was always ready to take the ball and became the 1968 World Series hero with three victories over St. Louis. *(Photo courtesy of Detroit Tigers)*

Denny McLain was brilliant on the mound, especially in 1968 when he notched 31 victories. Off the field, his antics led to heartaches for John Fetzer and baseball. *(Photo courtesy of Detroit Tigers)*

Mickey Stanley was a result of the productive farm system that picked up speed after John Fetzer purchased the Tigers. A native of Grand Rapids, Michigan, Stanley was a long-time fan favorite. *(Photo courtesy of Detroit Tigers)*

Jim Northrup was another product from the Tiger farm. He delivered the game-winning hit in the seventh game of the 1968 World Series against the St. Louis Cardinals. *(Photo by Thomas Donoghue)*

John Hiller demonstrated far more courage off the field than ever called for on the pitcher's mound. After fighting back from a career-threatening heart attack, the lefty became one of the premier relievers in history. *(Photo courtesy of Detroit Tigers)*

John Fetzer enjoyed a champagne shower in the Tiger lockerroom after Detroit's 1968 seventh-game victory over the Cardinals. *(Photo courtesy of Associated Press)*

Later, the Tiger players gave Fetzer a whirlpool bath. *(UPI/ Corbis-Bettmann)*

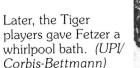

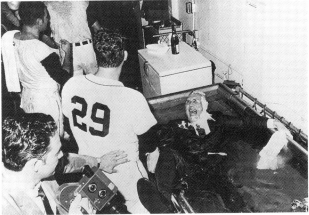

Al Kaline (right) represented the classic work ethic which John Fetzer believed was one of the game's inherent beauties. *(Photo courtesy of Detroit Tigers)*

For John Fetzer and Manager Mayo Smith (right), who guided the 1968 Tigers, the World Series trophy came to Detroit where it belonged. That magical year, which followed a summer of civil strife in 1967, was Fetzer's proudest. *(Photo courtesy of Detroit Tigers)*

John Fetzer and Hall of Fame former Tiger second baseman Charlie Gehringer (right) shared a number of similar qualities. Both were quiet, unassuming and exuded class. The two cherished each other's friendship from the moment Fetzer purchased the Tigers. *(Photo courtesy of Detroit Tigers)*

In September, 1969, the Tigers hosted a day to honor an unofficial all-time greatest Tiger team. John Fetzer is flanked by two stars who performed for him — Al Kaline and Denny McLain. Left to right: Hank Greenberg, Hal Newhouser, Billy Rogell, Kaline, Fetzer, McLain, George Kell and Charlie Gehringer. *(Photo courtesy of Detroit Tigers)*

Baseball is a game of strange partnerships. The volatile Billy Martin didn't seem to fit the Tiger mold. The peppery manager, however, did lead the Tigers to an East Division title in 1972 and Fetzer certainly appreciated Martin's baseball talents. *(Photo courtesy of Detroit Tigers)*

Fetzer called long-time Tiger President and General Manager Jim Campbell (left) his "most loyal employee." *(Photo courtesy of Detroit Tigers)*

Manager Ralph Houk led one of the most extensive player rebuilding projects in Tiger history. And he did it with class. *(Photo by Bill Gallagher)*

Alan Trammell spent his entire career with the Tigers, teaming with second baseman Lou Whitaker for a major league-record 18 seasons. Trammell was the picture of consistency and ideal work ethic, and was the MVP of the 1984 World Series. *(Photo by Clifton Boutelle)*

Nobody did it better than Lou Whitaker. "Sweet Lou" quickly moved through the Tiger farm system to become a major league star and spent his entire career with the Tigers. *(Photo by Clifton Boutelle)*

Sparky Anderson not only became John Fetzer's favorite manager, but was also one of the most popular managers in baseball history. Sparky finished as Detroit's winningest manager and ranks third in all-time baseball history. *(Photo courtesy of Detroit Tigers)*

John Fetzer served as baseball's unofficial conscience for more than two decades. Here he is flanked by American League President Lee MacPhail (left) and Commissioner Bowie Kuhn (right). Both sought Fetzer's insight for a variety of critical and sensitive matters. *(Photo courtesy of Detroit Tigers)*

Not only was Al Kaline the favorite Tiger player of John Fetzer ...
(Photo by Bill Gallagher)

... Fetzer was viewed with equal admiration by Kaline, as portrayed by the message No. 6 inscribed on this publicity photo. *(Photo courtesy of Fetzer Institute Archives)*

At this 1981 baseball luncheon in the White House, Fetzer is greeted by President Ronald Reagan. *(Photo courtesy of the White House)*

John Fetzer hand-picked Tom Monaghan (right) to purchase the Tigers and continue its history in the pure tradition of baseball. Witnessing the signing is long-time Tiger boss Jim Campbell. *(Photo courtesy of Detroit Tigers)*

John Fetzer spent many hours on the phone serving as counsel to fellow franchise owners and leaders of baseball. It was Fetzer's undying faith in the tradition of the game that served as a beacon through a volatile era. *(Photo courtesy of Detroit Tigers)*

Fetzer was inducted
into the Michigan
Sports Hall of Fame
in 1983. *(Photo
courtesy of Fetzer
Institute Archives)*

JOHN EARL FETZER
OWNER, DETROIT TIGERS, 1956 – 1983

HIS IMPACT ON BASEBALL WILL BE FELT FOR YEARS TO COME. A RADIO - TV
OWNER AND PART OF A SYNDICATE - PURCHASE OF THE TIGERS (1956) FROM
W.O. BRIGGS; BECAME SOLE OWNER, 1961. FOR LONGEST TENURE THAN ANY OF 5
PREVIOUS OWNERS OF THE TIGER FRANCHISE THAT ORIGINATED IN 1901;
FETZER'S OWNERSHIP PRODUCED 1968 WORLD SERIES TITLE OVER ST. LOUIS,
2ND PLACE (101 VICTORIES) 1961, AMERICAN LEAGUE EAST TITLE 1972,
BASEBALL'S THIRD-BEST RECORD (92-60) AMONG THE 26 TEAMS 1983; MEMBER
MAJOR LEAGUE PENSION COMMITTEE 1963-'64, MEMBER AL BOARD OF DIRECTORS
1965; MEMBER MAJOR LEAGUE EXECUTIVE COUNCIL 1960-'65, 1973, 1975-'79;
CHAIRMAN AL PLANNING COMMITTEE 1973. FOR YEARS CHAIRMAN RADIO-TV
COMMITTEE THAT ASSURES BASEBALL ITS LONG-TIME MEDIA SUCCESSES.
ELECTED TO MICHIGAN SPORTS HALL OF FAME 1984.

Fetzer helped cut the ribbon during the 1989 dedication of the Baseball Hall of
Fame's Fetzer-Yawkey wing. *(Photo courtesy of the National Baseball Hall
of Fame Library, Cooperstown, NY)*

CHAPTER 13

A House Divided

War between the owners and the major league players union seems to taint the game every few years.

Or maybe it's peace that periodically interrupts the war. In the world of big business baseball today, it's tough to tell the difference. Is the game passing through a little treaty of peace, or are the two sides just gathering ammunition for the next round of labor battles?

It doesn't seem to matter anymore. Modern fans have come to expect a disruption, or at least an assault of derogatory outbursts, from both sides every few years. It wasn't like that years ago. That alone doesn't make the past any better or worse than the present. It means simply that times were different.

Before the advent of player free agency, the only movement of players came at the discretion of the clubs holding their contracts. Players could be traded. They could be sold. They could be demoted to the minor leagues or they could be released from the organization altogether. But the player had no voice about where he might be playing the following season.

Then along came the free-agent revolution of the mid-'70s from which players were granted free agency and were backed by the courts.

History alone will judge whether the revolution was for better or worse. Only a fool would argue, however, that the game remains the same.

The game has changed in a number of ways. For the modern player, this is the best of times. Even the part-timer who spends most of the season sitting on the bench makes more money in one year than most average workers earn in a decade.

The average major league yearly salary now is more than $1.5 million. Now the highest paid player makes over $10 million a year.

Is it wrong? Obviously not. Or the owners would not be paying such unthinkable princely sums.

But the price for doing business in this fashion certainly has changed how baseball operates today. The sportsman/owner has become as much a part of history as Ted Williams and Mickey Mantle. The game is governed by some of the nation's largest corporations with franchises serving as tentacles of the octopus. And again, only a fool would argue that the game is still the same.

With this change in franchise ownership came revolutionary operational philosophies. No longer does the game itself remain the sole focus of activity at the park. Baseball now is filled with an endless array of marketing gimmicks that, at times, tax the patience of the purist who remembers how simply the game once was played.

The Tigers were late entries into the free-agent sweepstakes. They signed Tito Fuentes in a minor free-agent deal for the 1977 season. It wasn't until before the World Championship season of 1984 that they signed a major free agent in Darrell Evans.

It was John Fetzer who helped to seal the deal with a personal phone call to Evans. Fetzer explained that he did not object to signing a free agent who might help clinch a run at a pennant. He objected strenuously to frivolous spending in an attempt to buy a pennant. History has proven that pennants are rarely purchased.

Fetzer shared his thoughts about baseball's escalating salaries at a meeting of the Michigan Associated Press Sports Editors Association in 1980:

> Many clubs have committed themselves to salary policies which are completely unsound ... You can't blame the players for the situation that exists. If I were a player, I would try to go out and get exactly what they are. The players are saying, if the owners

are willing to pay us, they must have the money to pay us. Baseball had a stodgy development. Its growth pattern was not progressive. The game did not develop along the lines it should have to benefit the players. That's what helped Marvin Miller the most. But nobody expected the pendulum to swing so far in the other direction. And a few owners on ego trips and greedy to win now, no matter what the effects, are pushing that pendulum farther in the players' direction.

I am going to pay a player what he's worth, but I'm not going to pay players what these few ego-riders are paying them because they are not worth it. Those of us who have watched players with fat contracts have seen that they don't play up to the potential of what they did prior to the long-term contract. Fans are the first to know when a player isn't putting out and when he is. You can't have a ball club with a bunch of guys who are thinking more about money instead of baseball. Any franchise that believes in the fans, believes in what it is trying to do, can't afford to jeopardize that franchise with huge deferred contracts.

We're going to do everything we possibly can to hold on to the players we have. But we'll probably lose some. There's no way I can look into a crystal ball and see what will happen in the bidding. There's no way I can look into the crystal ball and say I will match dollars with the rest of the field. I have the wherewithal to do the matching, but in the long range, it would send this franchise down the drain, and I see that as a violation of public trust.

Fetzer, of course, believed in the traditional method of developing a ball club—building from within. He believed in scouting and signing good young talent. The talent then was nursed through the minor-league system before getting a shot at the major-league level. Fetzer felt the crafting of a homegrown unit provided intangible value to baseball and the community. Fans could then truly identify with players of their own organization.

"My position was clear and openly stated," Fetzer said. "I thought our game was headed toward serious trouble if we didn't have some kind of an orderly reserve system for players.

"I had great concerns that giving a player the freedom to jump from team to team in search of the check with the greatest number of zeroes on it was going to be detrimental to the game and to the fans. Fans identified with players because they could depend on the guy if he was the team's top gun. Worse than that, skyrocketing and uncontrolled salaries added up to increased ticket prices in my book, which violated my long-held belief that baseball had to remain an affordable family entertainment."

As Bowie Kuhn prepared to step down from his position as commissioner in 1984, he explained Fetzer's interpretation of free agency.

"His (Fetzer's) opposition to the free-agency concept was perceived by some to be a reflection of his conservative nature," Kuhn explained. "John's position was that baseball clubs would be wiser to concentrate on player development, that free agency was a 'fool's paradise.' As usual, John practiced what he preached, because he had great confidence in his own judgment. He demonstrated that you can operate successfully by concentrating on player development.

"His primary concern about the effects of free agency, namely the skyrocketing salaries, was that clubs would be taking on obligations that threaten their financial foundations. These ballooning obligations would be a millstone around the game's neck."

In 1976, author Harold Parrott examined baseball's ownership in a book called *The Lords of Baseball*. In it, Parrott concluded that baseball owners had to be bright or they couldn't have amassed the fortunes necessary to gain entry into the game. However, they failed to exercise the same good judgment when it came to matters of baseball. Parrott went on to single out Fetzer as the one owner who stood out above his peers. Parrott credited Fetzer with running the Tigers with decency and with a regard for the city in which they operated.

Fetzer's fears were certainly prophetic. The modern game seems to be more concerned with the construction of private corporate luxury suites in the park than it does with discovering a solution to various problems on the field.

"It is a sad thing to see what is happening because some owners, who are concerned and who love and respect the relevance of sports, are being literally forced out of the game," Fetzer commented before selling the Tigers.

Fetzer did not predict the end of baseball. In fact, he assured that because "baseball embodies some of the central preoccupations of that cultural fantasy we like to think is a significant part of the American dream," the game itself will not pass away.

He predicted, however, that it would undergo radical surgery to conform to America's corporate style of life.

"The sins of the total corporate practice, to some extent, can be laid at our door, which means retribution can become onerous, and we can pay a big price for our indiscretions," Fetzer said.

Until the 1994 player strike, which eventually led to the cancellation of the League Championship Series and the World Series, the most devastating labor dispute with the players association occurred in 1981. The 50-day player strike caused the cancellation of 714 games and resulted in a split season.

Tensions between ownership and the players association, of course, were stretched to the edge. The disunity among the owners caused as much grief to Fetzer as that from the labor faction.

There were hawks and doves among the owners. Some wished to settle the strike as quickly as possible regardless of consequences. Others preferred to entrench themselves for as long as necessary in an effort to break the spirit of the players association.

The disunity resulted in considerable confusion for the owners and their negotiating team. Sentiment became so chaotic, in fact, that some members of the American League threatened to resume their schedule even if the National League opted to keep the doors closed.

At one of the ownership meetings just before the strike was settled, Fetzer addressed his colleagues with a moving speech.

"It provided me with one of the most remarkable moments I have ever experienced," recalled former Baseball Commissioner Bowie Kuhn. "As usual, this was a particularly tough meeting. Everyone was irascible and nervous. Suddenly, John stood, walked up to the lectern very slowly and quietly said, 'I have something to say.'

"It went something like—'First, I want to say I've been in baseball a long time, involved with all you people, and I've come to know you well. If I have offended or hurt any of you, I want you to forgive me.' He then went on to say what he believed should be done to resolve the strike situation. It was a very moving experience, one that emphasized John's humility and spirituality. Others worked hard to settle the strike, but John may have ended it there."

Fetzer's speech focused on unity. The owners, regardless of their personal persuasions, had to remain united and support their own negotiating team.

"There were cracks appearing in our facade," Fetzer explained later. "A few even wanted to submit to arbitration, as if they hadn't already lost enough that way. I told them that we had to stand firm behind our Player Relations Committee because that's what we had chosen in good faith to do.

"Marvin Miller once said that we could put a coalition of 20 clubs together and they wouldn't have a chance because of six hard-liners who tell the others when to sit up, when to heel, and when to beg. I guess he counted me among the six. I didn't agree with him on that. I don't think I have ever imposed my will on anybody. I tried to reason and appeal to the others' good sense.

"I think it's absolutely wrong for anyone, whether in baseball or whatever else, to think that whatever is good for him has got to be good for the rest of the industry. I had an obligation as one of the leaders of baseball not to do anything that was going to hurt the overall structure of the game.

"If my crystal ball was worth much back then, I said that there had to be a change in the direction baseball was headed. Baseball could be a Garden of Eden for the owners, the players and, most importantly, the fans. We were about to take a big bite out of the apple."

Support was returned to the Player Relations Committee. Baseball paid an expensive price, but eventually agreement with the players association was reached.

"John's steadying influence kept everybody under control," recalled California Angels General Manager Buzzie Bavasi. "People were going off in all directions before that little speech of his. It went something like, 'Gentlemen, it's one for all and all for one.'

"John was a hard-liner when it came to the preservation of the game. Being from the old school, he had to take a hard line because he believed the new school was not necessarily better than the old school. But never did his hard line stance ever preclude him from listening to reason. He always listened to reason. I never saw him enter a meeting with a preconceived notion. He went in with an open mind and was willing to listen to all presentations. Certainly, he influenced the other owners, but never by force or threat."

If there was a single tangible factor that at least planted a seed to get Fetzer thinking about selling the Tigers it was the 1981 player strike. It was during that period that Fetzer could foresee the changes that baseball would soon undergo in order for survival. Operating costs would soon skyrocket out of reach of the traditional baseball franchise owner. Corporate takeovers were only a few years away.

Along with these changes came a shift in the traditional order of owner-general manager-manager-player leadership.

"If John were still with us today," Kuhn said, "I don't think he'd tolerate what's going on in the game. What's happened here is that there's been a fundamental shift of power away from owners and away from the commissioner to the players association.

"I think that John would have found it absolutely impossible to be comfortable in a world where the slugger says 'The heck with it, I'm not going to hit the ball to right to move the runners to second and third. I'm going to swing away.'

"The managers were losing control of the game. I think John would have found that impossible to deal with."

The player relations pendulum certainly had swung. There would still be a few more years for Fetzer to exert his influence; but disillusionment definitely had begun to take its toll.

CHAPTER 14

Flannel and Double Knits

I n baseball's "golden age" of the '50s and '60s, players sweated through steamy summers wearing flannel uniforms and wool caps. Their magnificence on the field was enough to mask any scars and sores that came from the administration of the game.

There were always problems. They just became bigger as the core of franchise ownership shifted from individuals to arms of corporate giants. As the ante for running a club continued to rise, so did the underside become more exposed.

Accordingly, the revolution in media coverage also had an effect on the game. Unlike today when the media devotes at least as much time and energy covering an endless array of off-field matters, there was a time when few fans really cared what went on behind the closed doors of a club's front office. Not as long as the men upstairs put players on the field who could spark a summer with a lot of wins. Or at least some hope for the future.

When John Fetzer took over the Tigers, it was a time to love or hate the Yankees. There was no in between.

Those were the days of Casey Stengel. While Casey mesmerized the nation with his peculiar charm, his boys were out plundering anyone in their way. There was Mickey Mantle, Yogi Berra, Roger Maris, Moose Skowron, Elston Howard, and a host of other muggers who feasted on American League pitchers as they bullied their way toward another World Series.

Fans from New York and sadists sprinkled around the country chuckled almost fiendishly at the beatings initiated by their boys from the Bronx. The rest of American baseball fans shared a common bond of hate for the Yankees. If a Detroit fan, for instance, couldn't have his Tigers win, then he pulled for the White Sox or Indians or Red Sox. Anyone except the Yanks.

Even when the Tigers didn't win, fans rallied behind their own favorite players. Those heroes came in all shapes and sizes. They had their own strengths. They were limited by particular weaknesses. Some players were very good. Others had to struggle just to stay in the American League.

But they all wore that old English "D" over their hearts on those creamy white flannels and later on the more comfortable double-knit jerseys. That made every one of them special. They all represented the spirit of Detroit.

Over the years of Fetzer's ownership, a collection of players captured the city's undying loyalty. There was Harvey Kuenn, tobacco-spitting champion who could send laser shot singles to all three fields after an all-night romp on the town. Rocky Colavito, matinee idol who contorted his neck violently before slamming another fastball into the leftfield bleachers. Jim Bunning, clubhouse lawyer who peppered management with player concerns before slipping his sidearm fastball past the most dangerous hitters. Frank Lary, the Alabama right-hander nicknamed "Taters," who made a career out of whipping the Yankees. Dick McAuliffe, who perspired like an assembly line worker at second base. Then he'd wipe the sweat from his forehead and rev up an emotional crowd with his high leg lift and a drive into the right field upper deck overhang to win a game in the last of the ninth.

There were countless colorful characters. Mickey Lolich with his neighborly potbelly. Mickey Stanley with his forever boyish grin. Gates Brown with his menacing scowl, twinkle in his eye and flair for late-inning heroics. Willie Horton with his tree-trunk arms, steel-vault chest and majestic home runs to every long-distance point of Tiger Stadium. Denny McLain whose off-field turmoil snatched a chunk of dignity from the game. Mark Fidrych who, for one glorious rookie season, talked to the baseball and stymied the most grizzly veteran hitters as he restored a sense of innocence to the game.

Of all the players to perform for Fetzer, one stood clearly above all else: Al Kaline, forever remembered simply as No. 6.

Kaline was the symbol of Fetzer's image of the consummate professional. Not only for his long list of Hall of Fame accomplishments, but more for the class and style he brought to the city with his work ethic, day after day.

Kaline joined the Tigers the day after graduating from Baltimore's Southern High School in 1953. He didn't strip the Tiger uniform from his back for the last time until 3,007 hits and 22 seasons later. He never really removed that old English "D" too far from his heart.

Kaline became the youngest player to win a batting title. He was only 20 when he captured the crown in 1955, the year before Fetzer bought into the Tigers. But it was Kaline's work ethic and overall class that still charms the city that worships him today.

Kaline was a special kind of player and special kind of man. In 1971, for instance, he turned down a $100,000 salary offer from the Tigers when that was the magic figure for players of superstar status.

"I couldn't take it," Kaline said, "because I didn't feel like I should be a $100,000 ball player. I hadn't had what I considered a good year in 1970. I felt they were just giving me the $100,000 because I'd been around for so long."

The similarities between Kaline and the city he represented were startling. He showed up ready to work every day. He was soft spoken. The biggest controversy ever to surround him was whether to bat him third or fourth in the lineup. He was, and remains, the traditional family man.

"I think Mr. Fetzer liked what I stood for and brought to the stadium every day," said Kaline, who still makes Detroit his home and serves as a commentator on the Tiger television network. "I was more his kind of guy."

Kaline's character meant a lot to Fetzer and the city. It was around the Hall of Famer that Fetzer had his teams constructed.

"Mr. Fetzer loved his players," Kaline recalled, "and the players loved him. But he made it a point not to hang around with the guys. He never came around the clubhouse all the time when we were winning like you see some owners do. He and Jim (Campbell) felt the clubhouse belonged to the players. They both felt that if you were going to hang around when the team was winning, then you better have the guts to be there when it was struggling."

George Kell played for the Tigers before Fetzer's ownership. Although he played for several teams in his Hall of Fame career,

Kell has always considered himself a Tiger. He was inducted into Baseball's Hall of Fame as a Tiger. It was directly because of Fetzer that Kell returned to the Tiger broadcast booth after stepping down for one season in 1964.

"Mr. Fetzer loved his players, but it was almost as if he didn't know them," Kell explained. "That's because he left the operation of the club up to the professionals who knew the game. He kept very much up to date with everything that went on with the team, but it was his philosophy to have a clear chain of command. He didn't need to boost his ego from hanging around with players."

Fetzer did not fraternize with the players. But he certainly expected his blueprint for the development of his Tigers to be followed. He never wavered from his belief that the Tigers must be developed by building from within their own minor-league system. And he believed equally fiercely in a well-designed organization that functioned professionally . . . and with class.

The fruits of that design speak for themselves in the overall performance of the entire organization throughout Fetzer's tenure.

Sticking primarily to the program of Fetzer's design, the Tigers consistently produced competitive teams. They didn't always win, but they did remain among the American League's upper echelon year after year.

When the yardstick for measuring financial success was drawing at least one million fans through the turnstiles, the Tigers set the standard. They hold the American League record for having done so each year since 1965. The 1968 Tigers were the first in franchise history to crack the two million mark.

Fetzer was candid that it was a ball club's responsibility to its fans to remain financially solvent. He was proud of annual Tiger attendance figures. It confirmed his belief that an organization had to remain fiscally sound to remain competitive. And the Tigers competed vigorously each year, primarily with players that the organization had originally signed.

"Mr. Fetzer wasn't frivolous with money," Kell said, "but he did whatever was necessary to keep the Tigers competitive every year. I remember Jim (Campbell) telling me so many times that Mr. Fetzer never wanted a minor-league team out on that field. He had too much respect for the working man. He would not allow Detroit fans to pay major league ticket prices for a team that couldn't compete. You can't get away with that in a workingman's town like Detroit. At least not with a clear conscience."

Because of Fetzer's philosophy of developing homegrown talent, memories of former players provide a pleasurable nostalgic trip through Tiger history.

The beginning of the '60s was a significant period for the construction of the Tigers under Fetzer. It was then that the foundation was laid for the ultimate success which was only a few years away.

By the beginning of the decade, the Tigers already had begun to form the nucleus around which they would build. The center was Kaline, already one of the American League's established superstars. With Kaline as the anchor, the Tigers went about filling in the pieces. A few of those players, in fact, already were being groomed in the Tiger minor-league system.

Shortly after Fetzer had purchased into the team, the Tigers signed pitcher Mickey Lolich, second baseman Dick McAuliffe, shortstop Ray Oyler and third baseman Don Wert.

The Tigers struck gold with their signings in 1960 and 1961. And most of the glitter came from right near home, outstate Michigan, in outfielders Jim Northrup and Mickey Stanley. Gates Brown was signed out of an Ohio prison and went on to become the most prolific pinch hitter in Tiger history.

In 1961, the Tigers completed two of their most significant signings. Off the campus of the University of Michigan came Bill Freehan. The baseball and football star from Royal Oak, Michigan became a perennial all-star behind the plate.

From the sandlots of Detroit, raised in the shadows of Tiger Stadium came Willie Horton. The burly outfielder became more than just one of the league's deadliest sluggers. He became a symbol of Detroit's black inner city. He also became one of the most beloved Tigers of all time.

"I wound up playing in a lot of cities," Horton recalled. "But Detroit was and always will be my home.

"There was something special about the Tigers back then. We were more than just a good baseball team. We were family. It started with Mr. Fetzer. A lot of people never knew how much he cared about the team.

"He cared about the fans. He cared about the whole city. He could have moved the team out of the city, but he knew where it belonged.

"We had a special feel that's hard to explain. We knew we couldn't win it all the time. But we always knew we were going to give the fans their money's worth. I was always so proud to wear that Tiger uniform. In my heart, I'll always be a Tiger."

As this nucleus matured, memories of a lifetime were created.

The first half of that decade was spent piecing together a championship team and establishing long-range stability in the front office. Campbell established himself as head of the entire operation. Behind Kaline, the players were falling into place, a few pieces each year.

Detroit's lone legitimate run for the pennant in that period occurred somewhat prematurely in 1961. Norm Cash struck gold in that compact left-handed swing to win a batting title with his .361 mark. He and Colavito combined as a lethal one-two punch to crunch 96 home runs. Coupled with the artistry of Kaline and the pitching magic of Jim Bunning, Frank Lary, Hank Aguirre and Don Mossi, the Tigers won 101 games to tie their then-club record.

The Tigers took the race into September. They were just one-and-one-half games behind New York. Then they were swept in a series by the Yankees and eventually wound up in second place, eight games behind.

It was the season Mantle and Maris trumped Cash and Colavito with 114 home runs. It also was the season that followed a winter of discontent for the Tigers.

Fetzer had to scurry to find a manager for his team. Joe Gordon had resigned after the 1960 season, primarily because of a difference of player philosophy with Bill DeWitt. Gordon wanted to bring up prospects from the farm. DeWitt wanted to stick with established players.

Fetzer already had removed DeWitt as president. He agreed with the idea of promoting his own young players. But now he was faced with finding the right manager to lead them.

After a failed attempt to persuade the legendary Casey Stengel to manage the Tigers, Fetzer settled upon unknown Bob Scheffing. And for the moment, it was the best decision he could have made.

Blending youngsters with experienced players, Scheffing led the Tigers through their most exciting summer since the club won the World Series in 1945.

Once the season ended, Fetzer himself became the biggest sports news story in Detroit. On November 14 he purchased the remaining 3,333 shares under the Knorr jurisdiction to become sole owner. One of the most visible changes for the fans was the changing of the park's name from Briggs to Tiger Stadium.

The next few years were dedicated to shaping the franchise according to the vision Fetzer believed worthy to carry the name of the Detroit Tigers.

The Tigers tumbled to fourth place in 1962. Maybe the team had over-achieved in its pennant run of 1961. Maybe some of the youngsters weren't quite ready to deal with the success they had somehow stumbled into one delirious summer before. But the loss of Kaline for 61 games certainly took its toll on an anticipated repeat run.

Ironically, the injury that sidelined the magnificent rightfielder occurred in Yankee Stadium, a familiar Tiger killer of dreams. While making a game-ending diving catch of a sinking line drive off the bat of Elston Howard, Kaline broke his collarbone.

Kaline's absence and Detroit's dive back into the reality of the American League standings were, of course, the most noticeable events of 1962. But Fetzer's most significant move that year occurred away from the shouts and excitement of a packed stadium. It happened in the quiet of the front office when he appointed 38-year-old Jim Campbell as general manager in mid-September. From then until his forced retirement in 1992, Campbell was the day-to-day boss of the Tigers as either general manager, president or chairman of the board.

And his peers, many of whom switched chairs a few times during his reign, all agreed there was none better.

"I guess I knew it was going to happen to Jim all along," Fetzer recalled. "In those early days of multiple ownership, he proved he knew more about baseball and the Tigers than anyone else. He had done everything. He was there all the time."

Campbell's first two years of leadership were anything but auspicious. After nine straight seasons of cracking the one million mark in home attendance, the Tigers drew a little over 800,000 in each of 1963 and 1964.

In 1963, the Tigers slipped under .500 for the first time in two years and the only time from 1961 through 1969. From friends and baseball executives in both leagues, however, Fetzer was apprised that his minor league system was loaded with budding talent. Through organization at the top and production from the farm, Fetzer was convinced the franchise finally was headed down the right path.

Lackluster play led to the June 19 firing of Scheffing in 1963. Campbell replaced him with veteran Charlie Dressen, who had led the Dodgers to pennants in 1952 and 1953 during their Brooklyn days.The plan was for Dressen to coax the most out of the team for the next couple of years until the wealth of Tiger farm prospects were ready to make their marks.

Dressen was the right man. But fate had other plans.

During spring training in 1965, Dressen returned to his California home suffering from heart pains. He remained there until shortly after Memorial Day when he returned to the team. During his absence, the club was handed over to third base coach Bob Swift.

In 1966, the Tigers were struck by one of the most eerie sets of circumstances in major league history.

On May 15 the Tigers were three games out of first place after defeating the White Sox, 8-6.Young prospects were developing according to plans.Everyone in the organization andTiger fans everywhere were convinced that the long-ago promised bright future was only a few steps away.

Not for Dressen, however. And not for the Tigers. On the following day, Dressen suffered a second heart attack. He never fully recovered and died on August 10 from a coronary arrest.

Swift again had replaced him as interim manager. Shortly after the All-Star Game, he was detected as having a tumor on his lung. He was replaced by Coach Frank Skaff. Swift never returned and died on October 17. Never in baseball history had two managers of one team died in the same year.

With prospects finally starting to blossom, the Tigers again were forced to search for a manager. Campbell's first choice was Al Lopez who had won two pennants and had ten second-place finishes in a 15-year career with the Indians and White Sox. Lopez was enamored with theTiger organization and all of its young players. But he finally decided not to join a new club.

Mayo Smith was hardly known when he landed theTiger job. By the time he left, however, he had taken the team to its most glorious year since World War II.

In 1967, Detroit was dealt a pair of crushing blows. Far more significant than anything that happened on the field were the civil riots that fractured a city in July.

Fires, looting, death and destruction spread throughout various areas of the city. National television reports likened certain parts of the city to the war being waged in Vietnam, a half a world away.

Fetzer offered to play some games behind locked doors at Tiger Stadium. He proposed to televise the games to help keep people inside their homes. Michigan Governor George Romney appreciated the offer but feared that the stadium lights might attract danger. The Tigers, therefore, moved a home series to Baltimore.

On the field, the Tigers continued to mature right before the eyes of their appreciative fans. This had now become a club of young veterans. Names like Kaline, Cash, Freehan, Lolich, Northrup, Stanley, Horton, Brown, McLain and others were to become permanently fixed in the memories of all Tiger fans. Maturity comes quickly in a race like the Tigers found themselves in.

The Tigers took the 1967 season down to the schedule's very last day. The Tigers hosted the California Angels in a doubleheader and needed a sweep to force a playoff with Boston for the right to meet the St. Louis Cardinals in the World Series.

Behind right-hander Joe Sparma, the Tigers won the opener, 6-4. But the final step remained as elusive as their unexpected pennant run of 1961. The Tigers dropped an 8-5 decision in the nitecap to finish in a second-place tie in the tightest race in American League history. The game and season ended abruptly when McAuliffe finished the ninth by grounding into a double play. Ironically, it was the only double play he grounded into all year long.

There were plenty of tears and broken hearts throughout the entire Tiger community. After the loss, Fetzer remained quietly in his private box at the park. He later returned to his office and composed a letter detailing the depth of his disappointment.

The redemption of the moment, however, was to be realized the following year. The Great Wall of China couldn't keep the Tigers from their destiny in 1968. After the bitter defeat of 1967, the maturation process was complete.

From the players on the field to the workers on every Detroit assembly line, a promise was made to play all the way into October the following year. The Tigers did more than that. Rallying from a three games-to-one deficit against the Cardinals, the Tigers charged to their first World Series Championship in 23 years.

The blood, the sweat, the tears and all the derision suffered until this moment of ultimate glory finally didn't matter.

Fetzer and the Tigers had devised a plan for a championship based upon building from within their system. They had stuck to it. Now it was time to celebrate.

"I remember what most baseball people had told me a few years prior," Fetzer said. "Everyone concurred that we had the best prospects around.

"I was supremely confident in them. So was Jim. I've always asked myself what would have happened if this bunch had failed. I always prided myself in hanging with a job until it was done. What if these guys had come up short? Would I have stuck it out? I really don't know. I only hope that I would have."

The question, of course, became moot. The Tigers, indeed, had reached baseball's ultimate plateau.

That magical "year of the Tiger" was crammed with memories that took on a life of their own. After some jockeying for position in the early weeks of the season, the Tigers took over first place on May 10. They never were seriously challenged.

McLain, of course, drew most of the national attention. He became the first major league pitcher to reach the 30-victory level in 34 years.

On the Tigers that year, though, everyone was a hero. Lolich displayed his usual workhorse reliability and posted 17 wins. Earl Wilson turned in 13 and Sparma added ten, including the 2-1 pennant clincher over the Yankees on September 17.

Horton led the Tiger power parade by slugging 36 homers. Freehan and Cash each belted 25, and Northrup chipped in 21, including four grand slams, two of them coming in consecutive at-bats on June 24 at Cleveland.

Injuries limited Kaline to 102 games. But he was steady with a .287 average. Quietly, Stanley had become one of the most brilliant centerfielders in either league. He made his biggest splash in the World Series when he was switched to shortstop and performed as if he had played the position his entire career.

It was a deliriously happy time. But the celebration was short-lived. The following year, the Tigers fell flat on their faces. They won a respectable 90 games, but still finished second, 19 games out of first place.

Maybe it was complacency. Maybe it was over-confidence. Whatever the reason, the Tigers tumbled hard.

After dropping to fourth place the following season in a year of McLain mischief and suspensions, the Tigers said good-bye to Mayo Smith and looked for a leader to regenerate a spark that had disappeared so quickly.

There have been more compatible matches. Most knowledgeable baseball people were skeptical from the start. For some
reason, perhaps only explainable by baseball's most faithful believers, fate coupled Fetzer and the Tigers with the volcanic Billy Martin.

Martin was brash. He was a time bomb waiting to explode.
He was as predictable as early season weather reports. His taste for
organization was similar to sucking on a freshly peeled lemon.

For a while, however, this unlikely match worked magic. In
his first year as manager in 1971, the fiery Martin rallied the Tigers
back to second place. The following year, the Tigers clawed their
way into the American League playoffs only to drop the series in
the deciding fifth game to Oakland.

The 1972 season was notable also for the comeback of 27-
year-old fan favorite John Hiller. The lefty established himself as
one of Detroit's all-time best relievers the following season. In 1971,
however, it looked like his playing career had reached a devastating end.

On January 11, 1971, Hiller suffered a heart attack. Scared
that his career was finished, he tried to keep his medical situation
secret from the club. In April, however, he underwent abdominal
surgery to bypass a certain part of the intestine that was producing
excessive cholesterol. He missed the entire season and half of 1972.
He returned with a rejuvenated baseball spirit and a fresh outlook
on life. For Fetzer, the Tigers and all baseball fans, it was a comeback that couldn't be measured by mere baseball statistics.

Martin vowed the Tigers would be back in contention in 1973.
The Tigers, in fact, made Martin's promise good as they clung to
first place in August.

But the team the Tigers had so patiently assembled years ago
was beginning to show its age. And Martin showed why his off-
field behavior kept knocking him out of jobs throughout his career.

"Between the foul lines, Billy was one of the best managers
around," Campbell said. "But there was a definite difference of opinion when it came to other matters."

Martin was fired near the end of the 1973 season. A new
rebuilding project was ready to begin.

"If a mistake had been made, it probably was that I had held
on to some of our older players one year too long," Campbell said.
"Those guys were special to the Tigers and special to our fans. We

had raised almost every one of them. I thought we could squeeze a little more out of them. I probably let my heart get in the way a little. I promised myself never to let that happen again."

Ralph Houk was Detroit's pick to lead this ambitious rebuilding project. It was tough and tiring. A lot of tears were shed before the job was finally finished. Many owners would not have had the patience to see the project through.

Again, the Tigers turned to scouting and development to repeat their success of the '60s.

Drafting players like Alan Trammell, Lou Whitaker, Lance Parrish, Jack Morris, Tom Brookens, Dan Petry, Steve Kemp and Jason Thompson among others, the Tigers clawed their way back to the top.

Fetzer and the entire organization realized there was no quick-fix solution. All were convinced, however, that this was the proper baseball way.

Houk was the grizzled World War II combat hero who came with the polish of the New York Yankees. He had played for them, managed them, and also served as the general manager before returning to the dugout for another stint as field boss.

Houk knew the game. He had long established his reputation both on and off the field. He had been toughened by every fastball and curve life had to offer.

He would need all his ammunition to tolerate the rebuilding project. It was his job to take all the bruises, barbs and bashings as the Tigers underwent one of their most extensive construction jobs in club history.

The Tigers were ready to unload the last remnants of their finest collection of talent. That talent had performed admirably and loyally. It simply became a matter of time.

Kaline persevered through the 1974 season in order to secure his lock on baseball immortality. Serving strictly as the designated hitter, Kaline passed the Hall of Fame automatic test by finishing his 22-year career with 3,007 hits. Five years later, he was a first ballot entry into Cooperstown.

After the team's second straight last-place finish in 1975, fan favorite Mickey Lolich was dealt to the Mets for slugger Rusty Staub. Piece by piece, the Tigers endured a mandatory dismantling. All the while, the Tiger farms were collecting talent for another run to glory.

It wasn't the best of times on the field. But the job was getting done according to all accepted standards of baseball tradition. In September, 1977, Trammell and Whitaker got their tickets to Detroit. They became keystone fixtures for the next 19 years. And with them came fulfillment of the promise that the rebirth had been finally put into place.

Houk nursed them into becoming regulars at shortstop and second base during the 1978 season. In September, Houk announced his retirement. They had been tough times for a tough leader. He had finished the job which the Tigers had asked of him.

"Forget the won-lost records under Ralph," Campbell said. "It was a time we all had to hitch up our belts and get the job done. Ralph knew what to expect. He had to get us through a tough time. He did it and never cried along the way. I don't know if anybody in the game could have done the job Ralph did. Ralph Houk was one of the finest men in baseball I ever had the privilege of knowing or working with."

Fetzer made refinements in the front-office operations. After promoting Campbell to president, he named long-time scout Bill Lajoie to vice-president of baseball operations. Prior to the historical season of 1984, Lajoie was promoted to general manager. One of his first significant moves was to sign free agent first baseman Darrell Evans who was the final touch on a championship infield. In spring training of that year, Lajoie traded for relief master Willie Hernandez and utilityman Dave Bergman to seal the magical run.

The Tigers promoted Les Moss from their Class AAA club to succeed Houk for the 1979 season. Moss was a tested and true soldier. He was in the right place, but at the wrong time.

Sparky Anderson was baseball's loveable white-haired leprechaun who charged to a national reputation managing the powerful Cincinnati Reds to two World Championships and a seemingly annual National League pennant in the 70s. After finishing second in 1978, the Reds stunned Anderson and baseball by handing him his pink slip.

Anderson did not start the 1979 season at the helm of any team. But in early June, several teams made overtures to lure him back into uniform.

Sparky was the last and most important piece of the puzzle Fetzer and Campbell were convinced was missing. On June 12, Sparky began a 17-year reign as manager of the Tigers. When he stepped down after the 1995 season, he had become Detroit's all-time winning manager and the third winningest manager in the history of the game.

"Les Moss would have made a fine manager," Campbell explained."He was a great baseball man and a real organization man. But when you have the chance to get someone like Sparky Anderson, you can't let that opportunity slip away. We knew we were on the brink of having a fine young team. And we knew Sparky was the man who could make it happen."

The bold and loquacious Anderson promised Detroit fans a championship within five years. The man of many words kept his promise.

After inching forward each season in Sparky's five-year plan, the Tigers completed the promise in 1984 with one of the most memorable seasons in the history of the game.

Not only did they lead the division wire-to-wire after a record-setting 35-5 start, they swept the Royals in the Playoffs and quickly won the World Series from the Padres in five games.

Fetzer had sold the club to Tom Monaghan after the 1983 season, but he remained with the club as chairman of the board. It was Fetzer's team and it provided a most appropriate final act for one of the most magnificent runs of ownership in baseball history.

Throughout all of Fetzer's years of ownership, it was the players who dictated the results on the field. They hit the home runs. They fired the shutouts. They rallied in good times and erred during the bad. But it was all done in pure baseball tradition. No player was bigger than the whole of the team. No individual precluded the strength of organization. This organization was a perfect reflection of direction and harmony of body, mind and spirit.

Those Detroit Tigers truly were John Fetzer.

CHAPTER 15

And Some Tears

Baseball is a game of the heart, maybe even more than one of physical skill. It touches all the senses. It touches every feeling.

Because of its nature, it induces delirious highs. The cost, of course, is paralyzing lows. They chisel at every emotion, leaving indelible scars. Nightmarish memories impossible to forget.

In no other business are feelings so disparate. It's part of the price each participant must pay.

During his three-decade reign of the Detroit Tigers, John Fetzer had his share of highs and lows. None of his other business successes could match those bubbling, floating, dreamy highs. The lows were devilish reminders of baseball's exacting toll.

A collapse of unity caused, in part, by the changing of franchise ownership created industry-wide heartache. So did the direction of player unionization, which eroded the essence of team concept. Those are setbacks from which the game is still reeling today.

For Fetzer, in Detroit, there were a few personal lows that were never reflected in team standings or failed pennant drives.

Fetzer's baseball agenda was predicated not only on what he could do for the long-range good of the game but also for the well being of the Tigers and the city.

It was something Fetzer refused to do, however, that perhaps resulted in his greatest gift to Detroit. Ironically, the ramifications of that decision provided him with one of his biggest disappointments.

Resisting the lure of a giant monetary windfall, Fetzer refused to move the Tigers from the core of the city to a new facility in the suburbs.

The hindsight—and insight—of history shows that from a strictly monetary standpoint, it was a bad business decision. In retrospect, it was a decision of the heart and not of the head. The decision was not based on dollars and cents. It was the type of baseball decision for which Fetzer exercised a particular set of values not governed by ordinary business principals.

"We had the opportunity to move the club to Oakland County where they were going to build a stadium for us," Jim Campbell said. "And the league would have approved the move because it still was within the community of Detroit. But Mr. Fetzer believed that baseball belonged in Detroit. And that's what kept them there."

The Detroit Lions, who rented Tiger Stadium from Fetzer for several years, of course, made the move to Pontiac's Silverdome.

Fetzer's decision to remain in Detroit was solidified after the Tigers won the World Series in 1968. He personally felt what the team meant to the city. The decision was based upon his belief that baseball must remain the game for the average working man.

"It was right then and there (1968), after seeing what this baseball tradition meant to a riot-scarred city, that I decided that the Tigers would stay in Detroit for as long as I owned the team," Fetzer said.

Over the years of Fetzer's ownership, there were moves to replace Tiger Stadium with a state-of-the-art facility in downtown Detroit. Fetzer supported the idea of a modern stadium for his Tigers. But for a variety of reasons, primarily political, the project never came to fruition.

Throughout his career, Fetzer had no choice but to weather the disappointments that accompany ownership of an institution like the Tigers. Few cut as deeply as the failed attempt to build that new park.

Although a project for building a new park is underway, Tiger Stadium still is an eight-and-a-half acre chunk of romantic baseball treasure. This charming double-decked structure remains a sculpted piece of baseball tradition. With Chicago's Wrigley Field, New York's

Yankee Stadium and Boston's Fenway Park, Tiger Stadium is a slice of Americana.

Walking through the stadium today, the baseball purist can almost hear the crowds from nearly a century ago. The ghosts of Ty Cobb, Charlie Gehringer, Babe Ruth and Walter Johnson seem to linger out on the diamond. Whispers from the past linger throughout the stands which nestle so close to the field. All the greats played there. Their presence remains.

Although the structure at the corner of Michigan and Trumbull didn't begin to take its present form until 1912, baseball actually has been played on the same site since 1900 when Detroit was in the Western League. The Western League was a minor league and was renamed the American League in 1901 when it was granted major-league status.

At that time, the wood-structured stadium was named Bennett Park in honor of Charlie Bennett, a popular Detroit catcher of National League days who was crippled in a freak streetcar accident.

In 1912, the Bennett Park stands were razed. A new concrete and steel structure was built at the cost of $300,000 and named Navin Field in honor of Tiger owner Frank Navin. The seating capacity was increased from 8,000 to about 23,000.

In 1924, the park was double-decked from first base to third base, increasing capacity to about 30,000.

In 1936 the rightfield pavilion and bleachers were also double-decked, increasing capacity to about 36,000. Two years later, the leftfield and centerfield stands were double-decked, increasing capacity to more than 53,000. The park was renamed Briggs Stadium in honor of owner Walter O. Briggs.

Since that time, the park has remained pretty much the same in appearance. In 1961, after Fetzer took control of the club, the park was renamed Tiger Stadium.

The romance, charm, beauty and tradition of Tiger Stadium still remains impossible to ignore. And long before contemporary commercial baseball dictated the need for ultra-modern facilities featuring luxury boxes, restaurants and every creature amenity short of private dressing rooms, Fetzer realized the importance of a new stadium to the Tigers and the community. But he remained adamant in his insistence that any new park be built in Detroit, preferably downtown.

"Baseball is a game of the working man," Fetzer explained many times, "nd certainly Detroit has always been a model of a working man's city. That's why as long as I had the privilege of serving as steward of the Tigers, the stadium was going to remain downtown."

For a while in the early '70s, it looked as if a new stadium was going to be built on the banks of the Detroit River, just south and east of Tiger Stadium.

Fetzer had pledged his support to the community effort. But the project was aborted by a Michigan State Supreme Court decision that kept the Tigers in their current home and eventually led to a renovation of the park.

The initial move for a new stadium dates back to 1966. In a January 6 letter to the Greater Detroit Board of Commerce, Fetzer endorsed the proposal.

"First, let me say that I, personally, as owner of the Detroit Baseball Club, and our organization as a whole are heartily in favor of a new stadium, subject to certain predetermined conditions which should and must be considered by all parties concerned," Fetzer wrote. "Out of necessity we must evaluate the situation as it pertains to the Baseball Club, not only from the standpoint of economics, but the future well-being of the Detroit Tigers as an institution and that of the general public in particular."

In the letter, Fetzer expressed his concern for the future of the game.

"To us," he wrote, "a stadium of the domed type should be a fundamental consideration. We believe that in the future, all stadiums in the northern part of the United States, where weather has become such an onerous problem, will ultimately be domed."

In the late '60s, the Wayne County Stadium Authority was formed to spearhead the construction of a new downtown stadium to house both the Tigers and Detroit Lions of the National Football League. Construction was to be financed primarily through the sale of bonds.

In 1970, Fetzer agreed to donate Tiger Stadium to a charitable purpose if the Tigers were provided a "satisfactory lease" on the new downtown stadium. Previously, the Tigers said they would have to be reimbursed for the existing stadium. The cost of that reimbursement was estimated to be between $1 million and $1.5 million.

In June 1970, the proposed new stadium looked as if it would be constructed only a few blocks east of the present park. By December, the site had been switched to the riverfront, just east of the convention Cobo Hall which sits on the river in the heart of downtown. The proposed stadium was to be a multi-purpose domed facility and cost approximately $150 million.

Fetzer endorsed the project. A December 20, 1970, editorial in the *Detroit Free Press* saluted his support:

"The support that John E. Fetzer, owner of the Detroit Tigers, has given to the building of a domed stadium on the riverfront should be decisive in getting the job done. Mr. Fetzer, as the owner of Tiger Stadium and the chief potential user, could probably have undermined the whole stadium effort had he imposed impossible conditions or set out to take his team to the suburbs."

However, even the best intentions were not good enough to get the project completed. After the Lions had decided to accept the invitation to move their franchise to suburban Pontiac and the Silverdome, the proposed downtown facility was struck down by a Michigan State Supreme Court decision.

In June, 1972, the Supreme Court upheld an earlier finding by Judge Blair Moody Jr., of Wayne County Circuit Court, that financial plans for the Detroit stadium were unconstitutional because they provided for using public money to build a stadium that would be used mostly for the benefit of a private business—the Tigers. The suit on which Judge Moody ruled was filed by Mayor Royce Smith of Belleville, Marc Alan, a Grosse Pointe investment counselor, and William Roskelly, a Redford Township civil engineer.

The ruling dealt a devastating blow, not only to the Tigers but also to the city of Detroit.

"There's not going to be any renegotiations of our lease," Fetzer said. "We have been very happy operating in Tiger Stadium. We can use that stadium for years to come."

In 1978, Fetzer sold the stadium to the City of Detroit for one dollar. He leased it back to the Tigers on a long-term arrangement after the promise of a multi-million dollar renovation plan was approved through the sale of bonds. Regardless of all the failed stadium attempts, Fetzer never once threatened to move his team from Detroit.

While the failure to realize a new stadium for the Tigers resulted in one of the biggest disappointments in Fetzer's baseball career, it didn't cut as deeply to the heart as the one he had endured only a few years prior.

The stadium, after all, was a mere business setback. It could be measured in dollars and cents, both to the city and the Detroit

Tigers. What hurt Fetzer more couldn't be measured in monetary terms. It cut at the core of the game's integrity. It was the entire Dennis Dale McLain debacle.

"I lost more hours of sleep over McLain than any other matter I had been associated with during the course of my career," Fetzer confessed.

McLain was a contradiction of near immeasurable proportions. On the mound he was a poet with the baseball. Off the field he became one of the most celebrated walking death wishes to blot baseball in the last half century.

All the brilliance McLain flashed on the mound was dulled by the shadows he cast away from the park. Those off-field escapades eventually led him to prison.

"John tried to cloak his disenchantment, but the whole Denny McLain affair had to have broken his heart," said former Baseball Commissioner Bowie Kuhn, who suspended the miscreant pitcher three times.

Fetzer's heart was broken because the McLain affair undermined baseball's foundation of integrity. The symbol that represented all that is good in our society had been publicly besmirched.

Kuhn concisely detailed the events that led to the most celebrated suspension until Pete Rose was banned from baseball, also for charges revolving around gambling, more than two decades later:

On February 19, 1970, I suspended Denny McLain from all organized baseball activities pending the completion of further investigation and my review of the facts. I based the initial suspension, substantially, upon certain admissions made candidly to me by McLain. These admissions related to his involvement in purported bookmaking activities in 1967 and his associations at that time.

My investigation has continued since that date regarding McLain's activities in 1967 and in subsequent years. I am satisfied at this time that my investigation has been thorough and has developed all pertinent information presently available.

"In January, 1967, McLain played an engagement (as an organist) at a bar in Flint, Michigan, and there became acquainted with certain gamblers, said to be involved in a bookmaking operation. McLain at that time commenced placing basketball bets with this operation, and subsequently he was persuaded to make financial contributions totaling approximately $5,700.

While McLain believed he had become a partner in this operation, and he has so admitted to me in the presence of his personal attorney, it would appear that he was the victim of a confidence scheme. I would thus conclude that McLain was never a partner and he had no proprietary interest in the bookmaking operation.

The fair inference is that his own gullibility and avarice had permitted him to become a dupe of the gamblers with whom he associated. This, of course, does not remove the serious dereliction on McLain's part of association with the Flint gamblers.

A thorough investigation has not revealed any other material facts beyond those I have described. There is no evidence to indicate McLain ever bet on a baseball game involving the Tigers or any other team.

There is no evidence to indicate that McLain gave less than his best effort at any time while performing for the Tigers. There is no evidence that McLain in 1967 or subsequently has been guilty of any misconduct involving baseball or the playing of baseball games.

McLain's association in 1967 with gamblers was contrary to his obligation as a professional baseball player to conform to high standards of personal conduct, and it is my judgment that this conduct was not in the best interest of baseball. It therefore must be made the subject of discipline.

In reaching my conclusions, consideration has been given to the fact that no evidence has been developed by my investigation that McLain's conduct, apart from his 1967 associations, have been inconsistent with his duties and obligations as a baseball player.

While it was true that in 1967 and subsequently, McLain has been irresponsible in his personal financial affairs, and that this is a source of serious concern, I have not in this particular case based my disciplinary action on such irresponsibility, although the probationary aspects of my action are related.

Under the circumstances, it is my judgment that McLain's suspension should be continued to July 1. In the meantime, his disassociation from all organized baseball activities must continue. In addition, McLain will be placed on probationary status, and be required to provide this office periodically with such data on his financial affairs as may be requested . . . to satisfy this office that personal financial irresponsibility will not again contribute to leading McLain into such a situation as involved him in 1967."

McLain was a bon vivant character who had established himself as one of the American League's finest pitchers in the second half of the '60s. From 1965 through 1967, he totaled 53 wins for the Tigers.

He had baseball marching to the snap of his fingertips in 1968. He led the Tigers to their first pennant in 23 years by becoming the first pitcher since Dizzy Dean in 1934 to win 30 games in the regular season. McLain finished with a remarkable 31-6 record and 1.96 earned-run average. He followed that season by leading the American League with a 24-9 mark to capture his second-straight Cy Young Award in 1969.

But the wildness McLain so masterfully controlled on the mound couldn't be contained once he left the ball park. News of the suspension and McLain's off-field activities sent shock waves through the entire sporting community. It was precisely the type of activity that ran contrary to the behavior Fetzer expected from anyone blessed enough to participate in major league baseball.

Suspicion of McLain's shady activities dated back to spring training of 1967. It was then that Doug Mintline, a sports writer for *The Flint Journal*, reported to Tiger General Manager Jim Campbell that he had overheard McLain place a bet on a college basketball game over the phone from the Tigers' clubhouse.

McLain was summoned to Campbell's office. He admitted to Campbell, executive consultant Rick Ferrell and Manager Mayo Smith to gambling on basketball and the horses. But he denied ever placing a bet on baseball games. Campbell instructed Smith to be particularly vigilant regarding McLain's activities.

After the Tigers won the World Series in 1968, Campbell was contacted by Tom McKeon, an attorney in charge of the United States Department of Justice Task Force investigating crime in the Detroit area. McKeon informed Campbell that he wished to have the F.B.I. meet with McLain about possible gambling activities.

The meeting took place on November 29 at Tiger Stadium. After the meeting and further investigation, no charges were leveled at McLain.

Fetzer and Campbell wanted to inform the Baseball Commissioner of the occurrence. However, the Tigers had been assured by McKeon that the questioning had nothing to do with baseball. After receiving cooperation from McLain, McKeon considered the matter closed.

While the 1969 season was productive on the field for McLain, off the field his life was starting to run totally out of control. McLain began to spend money far quicker than he could make it. He was investing in a variety of businesses that led to his financial insolvency. When he switched agents and his new representative, Ed May, wanted to purchase McLain's baseball contract, the Tigers immediately informed the Commissioner. The Tigers, of course, were informed that McLain's baseball contract must remain the exclusive right of the club.

All the while, the three-year investigation by the task force on gambling in the Detroit area had continued. Later, it unfolded evidence of McLain's possible involvement as a bookie.

The Tigers had been charged by certain members of the media of trying to cover up McLain's gambling ties, and nothing could have been further from the truth. The Tigers had meticulously followed the directions of the U.S. Attorney's Office and that of the Baseball Commissioner until all evidence had been gathered.

Following McLain's 1970 suspension, Fetzer personally wrote a chronicle of all the bizarre events surrounding his prize pitcher. It was partially in response to a segment of the media which charged that the Tigers had conducted an attempt to cover up McLain's actions. Fetzer wrote in part:

> Many people have been puzzled over the fact that officially the Detroit club has made no attempt to refute many of the misstatements of fact that have been evident on every side. We should like to respond by saying that our silence was due to the fact that, first, we did not want to prejudice in any way the acquisition of the facts in the Denny McLain case. We did not wish to hamper the work of all authorities who were pursuing that problem. Secondly, we were requested by the Commissioner of Baseball not to respond for the reason that he wished to maintain an environment that would be conducive to impartial investigation rather than a posture of charges and countercharges....
>
> This leads me to that which I believe to be a larger question concerning the Tiger organization and its relationship with the mass media. We have been pleased and are most grateful for the support we have had from the majority. We have no desire to enter into controversy with our many friends in the press, radio and television. However, since the suspension of McLain, some members of the fraternity have falsely charged the Detroit Club with being completely indifferent and incompetent, that we cov-

ered up facts, that we were lending money to McLain to pay his gambling debts, that we were racists, that we were bigots and a variety of other reckless and ill-founded allegations. In fact the situation became so low that a New York writer did a rarity when he took sharp exception to the shoddy reporting of this minority group. I think the Detroit club deserved better billing . . . .

However, let me make it clear that my concern is not with the mundane idiosyncrasies of living in a glass cage. My concern is with those deliberate and malicious chronicles that are designed by the few to create havoc and injustice to a time-honored institution. Such viciousness in our environment calls for the recipient to maintain a dedication of purpose, money and properties that is rare, indeed, in the human equation."

In other words, Fetzer was unafraid to take his share of hits from the media, even if he felt they were misguided. But he was not going to allow the Tigers or baseball to suffer more humiliation than the McLain affair already had exacted.

McLain's career continued to spin out of control even after his suspension. It seemed as though fans needed a scorecard just to keep up with the pitcher's on-again, off-again status.

Less than two months after his reinstatement, McLain was suspended again. This time it was for dousing two sportswriters with buckets of water before a Tigers home game. Seven days later, Kuhn added another suspension. McLain had gone beyond buckets of water. The last suspension was for carrying and brandishing a gun in a Chicago restaurant, according to the commissioner's office.

"I must say something about the character of John Fetzer and Jim Campbell," Kuhn said. "I suspended their star pitcher three times during one season and they never whined about it. That's the type of baseball men they were. That's the type of character they possessed. Even though it hurt them, they knew what was right."

After the 1970 season, McLain was involved in a multi-player trade that landed him in Washington. Three players—pitcher Joe Coleman, shortstop Eddie Brinkman and third baseman Aurelio Rodriguez, who went to Detroit in the deal—helped get the Tigers into the 1972 American League Championship Series.

McLain had left his mark on Detroit both on and off the field. Along with all Tiger fans, Fetzer appreciated the brilliance of his pitching mastery. But McLain's inability to appreciate baseball's inherent morality resulted in one of Fetzer's most painful experiences in the game.

There would be more. Some just hurt a little more than others. None, though, stung as hard as the one created by Dennis Dale McLain.

CHAPTER 16

Champagne and a Sigh of Relief

Winning a World Championship may be easier than describing the ecstasy of victory.

For the player, there's an instantaneous rush, like millions of exploding bubbles fighting each other to escape from a shaken bottle of champagne.

For the fan, there's an overwhelming surge of pride. Not only in his loyalty to the team, but also in the community at large.

For the owner and all of the team's workers behind the scenes, there's a sense of relief. What if all the weeks of preparation had not been good enough? Finally, everyone is free to surrender all their fears of failure.

That's the way it's supposed to be. It's a time to celebrate. It's a time to be proud. Above all, it's a time to give thanks.

Few are privileged to share in that maddening euphoria that only winning a World Championship brings. Many owners, players and executives spend careers in a sport only to walk away without ever getting a shot at their one moment of sports immortality.

Under Fetzer, the Tigers were privileged to share in two such celebrations. There was more to those victories than the gold trophies that accompanied them. More than all the accolades of a nation. More than a litany of praises from an often cynical media.

The victories of 1968 and 1984 paid tribute to the game's underlying foundation. The nucleus of both teams had been born and cultivated almost totally from within the Detroit Tiger system. First, young players had been scouted and signed. They were developed on the Tiger farms, then given a chance to excel in the big time.

Neither team blew the opportunity.

"Winning the World Series both times was the culmination and celebration of our overall philosophy," Fetzer explained. "We had constructed both those teams right from the roots."

It can be argued, of course, that those were the days—especially 1968—before player free agency helped to re-shape the direction of the game. Obviously all teams had to be built from within.

It can also be argued, however, that free agency always existed . . . only in reverse. It was totally controlled by the owners instead of the players. Wealthy teams, prior to player free agency, unscrupulously flashed their power. Many tried to buy themselves a championship through the purchase of players from the less affluent franchises.

Times, of course, changed. Now players dictate the directions of their careers. But the purity of baseball tradition lies in the crafting of a champion from within.

The 1968 team, admittedly Fetzer's favorite, was a blueprint of self-craftsmanship. It symbolized all of Fetzer's baseball ideals. The 1968 championship justified Fetzer's perseverance through those early turbulent years. It also kept him from making a decision he never wanted to face.

"Most baseball people in both leagues believed we had the best prospects around," Fetzer said of his organization in the early '60s. "I was supremely confident in them. So was Jim (Campbell)." The 1968 club was a workmanlike product sculpted in the workingman's capital of the country.

Before that glorious season, the team already was stocked with players who were regarded as having become part of every Tiger fan's family.

A generation of fans already had grown under the poetry of Al Kaline. Willie Horton was signed out of a Detroit ghetto after establishing himself as a sandlot legend on dusty diamonds only walking distance from Tiger Stadium. Bill Freehan was signed out of the University of Michigan. Mickey Stanley and Jim Northrup were signed from cities in the western part of Michigan.

Players like Mickey Lolich, Dick McAuliffe, Don Wert and Joe Sparma had worked their way through the Tiger system.

Gates Brown capitalized on his once-in-a-lifetime opportunity. He signed a contract while serving time in an Ohio prison and went on to become one of the most popular Tigers ever to wear the uniform.

Even some of the 1968 stars who came from other teams were indirect results of the Tigers' overall system. They had been acquired through trades for players originally signed by Detroit.

"Actually, the road to the championship began in 1961," Fetzer explained. "At that time we made a critical examination of the Tiger system from top to bottom. We analyzed our talent situation. We took a long look at the managers of our farm clubs. We went over our scouting personnel with meticulous care and made a complete study of all the elements required to put together a complete working force.

"We compared what we had at that time with the best of other major league clubs. We found that our system had the ingredients for success, but was somewhat lacking in the field of job classifications. There was a lack of coordination and a poor system of communications."

It took seven years before the champagne corks finally popped. For Fetzer and the entire Tiger organization, all the pain was worth the sacrifice.

"We created teamwork in the front office, teamwork in the farm system and teamwork on the playing field of Tiger Stadium," Fetzer said. "Unless teamwork starts at the top, it never will show itself on the field. What we saw in 1968 was a result of seven years of toil and sweat."

That moment was meant to be shared by all. Every fiber of glory belonged to each fan who has ever bled for the Tigers. It didn't matter whether it was long before 1968 or now, three decades later.

"Think what it (championship) means to our fandom in Michigan, Northern Ohio and Indiana, because there, alone, we have created approximately eleven million new managers of the ball club," Fetzer said after the victory.

"They not only manage the ball club, but they own it—lock, stock and barrel. It's their ball club and, right now, let no man try to take it away from them."

The 1968 Tigers were a team that took one championship season a step beyond all the glories of the game.

On the field, the season belonged to the Tigers alone. The passion of 1968 got its start at the end of the 1967 campaign when the team finished tied for second in the closest four-team finish in the history of the league. When the Red Sox clinched the pennant on the season's final day, the Tigers quietly promised themselves that no human force could possibly prevent them from playing in October the very next year.

They had become possessed. Almost from the start of the season, the Tigers actually toyed with the rest of the league. After moving into first place alone on May 10, they never surrendered the lead. They built their cushion to 13 1/2 games and finished the year 12 games in front.

The Tigers were masters of the comeback. Almost daily, a new Lazarus stepped forward to rally the team late in a game.

It was the "year of the pitcher" when the American League finished with a 2.98 ERA. The Tigers ranked third at 2.71. They finished on top with 59 complete games. The leader, of course, was the miscreant McLain. The rapscallion right-hander turned back the clock 34 years. He became the first major-league pitcher to notch 30 victories since Dizzy Dean in 1934. McLain won the first of back-to-back Cy Young Awards by going 31-6 with a 1.96 ERA.

A member of the 1968 Tigers and later long-time coach was Dick Tracewski. He had been the roommate of Sandy Koufax when the Hall of Famer, for a few seasons, established himself, arguably, as the best pitcher in history.

"Sandy was awesome," Tracewski said. "When he took the mound, he absolutely dominated every hitter. We always felt that if we could get him just one run, we had a chance to win the game.

"But for just one season, I can't believe I've ever seen anything like McLain in '68. He had something special about him. I can't explain it. When it was his turn to pitch, we knew we were going to win. I never had that feeling ever before in my whole career."

Lolich contributed 17 wins. Earl Wilson chipped in 13. But the eyes of a nation focused on McLain every time he touched the ball.

Horton powered the Detroit attack with 36 home runs. Cash and Freehan each popped 25 and Northrup delivered 21. Kaline was sidelined by injuries for a significant portion of the year, but his presence always was a weapon. He proved it in the one World Series of his career by playing every game and batting .375.

Kaline got the chance to shine when Manager Mayo Smith made one of the boldest moves in World Series history even before it began. Smith moved Mickey Stanley from centerfield to short-stop. Northrup replaced Stanley in center and Kaline provided more punch to the lineup by going back to right.

"Mayo laid his neck right on the chopping block," Campbell said. "I guess we all did. There we are in St. Louis. Lou Brock up to start the game. Wouldn't you know it? He hits the ball right at Mickey. He fields it and throws him out. That broke the pressure quite a bit. Mickey was a cool customer, but he was on pins and needles that day. If it had been a tough play and he'd kicked it, that could have screwed up the Series for him and us right there."

An iffy hunch turned into a stroke of genius. The Cardinals, though, were in for yet a bigger surprise.

While McLain drew center stage on the strength of 31 victories, Lolich became the ultimate scene-stealer. The rubber-armed lefty won three starts, including Game 7 as he outdueled the deadly Bob Gibson with a complete game effort. The Tigers were only the second team in history to rally from a deficit of three-games-to-one.

Even before the Series, the Tigers had cast a spell over the entire state. They drew a club record 2,031,847 in home attendance.

It culminated on that fateful October Thursday in St. Louis. But throughout that magical summer, a baseball team had helped to soothe a situation that the National Guard and state militia couldn't only a year before.

The social significance of a successful ball club often is ludicrously exaggerated. For the most part, success is shared by the players and the people who sign their checks. This year was different. This year success truly belonged to a community come together.

Historians have suggested it's impossible to explain the phenomenon of the '60s. If you weren't part of it, don't even try to understand. The same can be said about the impact of the 1968 Tigers. What that whole season meant to a crippled community may never be totally appreciated.

It was a time of conflict. A time of confusion. The nation was divided on a war being fought half-way around the world. Vietnam had sliced into the American spirit like no other conflict since the Civil War. Demonstrations protesting the war raged across the country. They were staged in front of the White House lawn. They were staged in almost every large and small city from East Coast to West.

Detroit was tangled in a war of its own. The race riot of 1967 was the nation's deadliest. Buildings were bombed, businesses were looted, blood flowed freely over the streets and lawns of the inner-city. Even today, remnants of the riot still stand rotting. They are ugly reminders of an unresolved hate.

For that one glorious summer, however, racial harmony had tenuously returned. It would be foolish to suggest that the Tigers had knit a lasting unity, but whatever small part they played, a whole nation was appreciative.

"I'll tell you how much that 1968 team meant to me and the city," Fetzer said. "I remember being in the clubhouse after the seventh game. It was pandemonium. There's no feeling in sports like winning a World Series.

"I grabbed Mayo Smith and hugged him. 'You not only won a World Series . . . you may have saved Detroit, too.'

"I think it was right then and there, after seeing what this baseball tradition meant to a riot-scarred city, that something snapped in my brain. The Tigers would stay in Detroit for as long as I owned the ball club. The bitter defeat of 1967, and then the flip side of the total victory of 1968—that's all part of it."

The World Series comeback ignited another commotion back on the streets of Detroit. This time, however, it signaled the sweetness of shared victory. The championship crown belonged to the whole community. At least for the moment, the shame of a summer just one year before was swallowed by the pride of a city come together.

Because of the throng of waiting frenzied fans, the Tigers diverted their victory flight from St. Louis. Instead of landing at Detroit's Metropolitan Airport, they switched to Willow Run, located in Ypsilanti just east of Ann Arbor. By the time they finally reached Tiger Stadium, more than 100,000 people crammed the narrow streets of downtown.

Horns blared; music was deafening. Above all the racket, human voices could be heard. These weren't shouts of hatred; they were the joyous screams of a kindred spirit.

On the streets of Detroit, blacks danced with whites. Each took turns swigging beer and wine from shared bottles. The Tigers were World Champions. It was a time when all were one.

Just the previous summer, Michigan Governor George Romney had been busy assisting the National Guard quell bloodshed on the streets. Now he sent a message to Fetzer. It was a letter Fetzer treasured until the day he died.

"The deepest meaning of this victory extends beyond Tiger Stadium and beyond the sports pages, radio broadcasts, and the telecasts that have consumed our attention for several months," Romney wrote.

"This championship occurred when all of us in Detroit and Michigan needed a great lift. At a time of unusual tensions, when many good men lost their perspective toward others, the Tigers set an example of what human relations should really be."

The outpour of congratulations was overwhelming. The messages were not obligatory. They came from the heart.

"Your fighting, winning team is the best tonic Detroit could have," wrote Henry Ford II, Ford Motor Company chairman of the board.

The baseball lords finally had their chance to thank the man who had given the game so much.

"This must be a rewarding experience," wired Pirates' Owner John Galbreath, "and in some measure repays you for your outstanding contributions to baseball."

League officials conveyed congratulations.

"I do not recall a more popular victory," wrote Paul Porter, counsel for the Commissioner's Office. "Even our friends in the National League conceded that if they had to lose, they would prefer that it be to the Tigers. This, John, is a genuine tribute to the stature which you have achieved in baseball and the personal affection and esteem your leadership has commanded."

And from John McHale, then president of the Montreal Expos and a friend who could appreciate the labor involved with putting all the pieces together, came this note:

"Your enjoyment in winning it all came through loud and clear on the TV screen after the seventh game. You turned it all around and made a championship organization out of a pretty big mess."

The championship of 1984 was not as socially significant as the one of 1968. But as Fetzer began his walk away from the game, it was equally gratifying.

Just as the first championship team, the 1984 version was basically home made. Except for first baseman Darrell Evans, who became Detroit's first major free agent signing, the team had been assembled in traditional baseball fashion.

It was Fetzer, in a personal phone call to Evans a few weeks before Christmas in 1983, who convinced the slugger to join the Tigers. For Fetzer, the deal made good business sense.

"There's a time to buy free agents and a time you don't buy them," he explained. "You don't buy them when you're building a young ball club. Once we got the nucleus, Evans was worth the gamble. And not for only what he did on the field. He was a steadying influence on all of our players. Right after my phone call to him, I thought we could win."

The Tigers had a barrelfull of rising stars who had worked their way through the system. Alan Trammell, Lou Whitaker, Lance Parrish, Kirk Gibson, Jack Morris, Dan Petry, Tom Brookens. The Tigers completed their roster by acquiring players through trades of other home-grown talent.

When Sparky Anderson joined the Tigers as manager in 1979, he predicted a pennant within five years.

Sparky made his prediction good. Fetzer and Campbell had been confident that the selection of Sparky five years previously was a baseball and business move they could not afford to let slip away.

"Perhaps it isn't quite proper to select one manager over another," Fetzer said. "At the time of each man's service, we felt we had the right man for the job.

"I will say that Sparky was very special. With all due respect to the rest, I would have to say he was my favorite. He knew the game extremely well. And there was this very special exuberance about him. He had the ability to lift the spirits and efforts of everyone around him. He is, no doubt, headed for the Hall of Fame."

Sparky's affection for Fetzer is reflected in his interpretation of what his boss meant to the game.

"What you have to understand about John Fetzer is that he was an owner who knew more about the game than any of the others," Anderson said. "What I mean is that he knew how to get the right baseball people and then step back and let them do their job. That sounds simple, but that's why he was so successful in everything he did. He never was worried about going around and trying to grab the spotlight from anybody. He knew who he was. He didn't need all that other stuff. All that other stuff is for the guys who aren't confident and don't feel good about themselves. Mr.

Fetzer was a real man. And he treated all of his people like real human beings. What you've got to understand is that the days of owners like John Fetzer are over. We were blessed for many years. It's a different game now."

Monaghan, who had purchased the club after the 1983 season, was living a dream throughout 1984. He was learning the game while Fetzer and Campbell called the shots. While maintaining an interest in the club, Fetzer had agreed to remain as chairman of the board for the next five years.

The 1984 Tigers made a mockery of the American League race. They started the season with nine straight wins. The fourth victory was a 4-0 no-hit gem by Morris in Chicago. They set a major league record by winning 35 of their first 40 games.

They led wire-to-wire and probably could have gone on to win the Super Bowl if they had continued playing.

The Tigers swept three games from the Royals to win the American League Championship Series. After splitting a pair of games in San Diego, the Tigers returned to Detroit to take three straight from the Padres and the World Championship trophy.

Just as in 1968, congratulatory messages poured in from all parts of the country. There was one from Detroit that touched Fetzer most. It came from Martin Hayden, retired publisher of *The Detroit News*. Hayden wrote:

My beef is aimed at my old profession and, more specifically the young print and broadcast 'experts' for not explaining how it all happened. They are lavish in praise of most everybody: Sparky, the playing stars, Roger Craig and even (sometimes) Jim Campbell. All rate their plaudits, but I get apoplectic at the rare mention that it was John Fetzer who made it all possible. Most specifically, I almost upchuck when some of these sports historians infer that all the good suddenly started flowing from the changed policy of the 'new owner.'

All of the above is a too verbose way of saying that a lot of us recognize what came from yours and Jim's policy of slowly building through the tough years, while aiming and planning for the climax of last Sunday afternoon.

Maybe yours is the undeserved fate of a 'laid-back' owner, who doesn't come running every time someone turns on a TV light. But I admire your modest approach, and want to go on record with my recognition of what you did for the Tigers and the perpetuation of their tenancy in downtown Detroit. To me the greatest thrill of all came from the fact that it all happened just before you officially bowed out.

Trammell was named the Most Valuable Player of the Series. After the season, Sparky won the American League Manager of the Year Award. Reliever Willie Hernandez made a clean sweep by grabbing the American League Most Valuable Player and the Cy Young Awards.

The euphoria of a World Championship carried the loyal Tiger fans throughout the winter. But Fetzer was wary.

"I had a feeling that the stuff I had been reading all my life about getting to the top not being as tough as staying there was really true," Fetzer said. "The only negative thing about our ultimate success in 1984 was the impression among fans and the writers that this was the first of a string of many."

It was dangerous thinking. Not only had baseball operations undergone radical changes, so had the players.

Only a day before winning the Cy Young Award, for instance, Hernandez threatened to leave Detroit if certain contract demands weren't granted.

Gates Brown resigned as batting coach after calling the club's 1985 salary offer "a slap in the face."

Looking through the window from the outside the picture couldn't be prettier. Once inside, though, things weren't quite as neat as they appeared.

"I felt sorry for Tom (Monaghan) because in his first year in baseball, the world was at his feet," Fetzer said. "His first assumption had to be, and rightfully so, was 'Why can't it be golden like this every year?'

"Jim (Campbell) and I could tell him that the fun had gone out of baseball as far as we were concerned. But Tom wouldn't understand.

"Before the union and the agents, you felt as if you were all on the same team. I think the 1984 Tigers came about as close to achieving that kind of feeling all up and down the line as anybody in the modern era of baseball."

Then it was gone. And after a few more years of serving as the Tigers' chairman of the board, so was Fetzer.

Baseball truly had changed. It still, arguably, is America's finest game. There is no arguing, however, that it will never be the same.

CHAPTER 17

The Perfect Goodbye

So often in the theater, the manner in which an actor leaves the stage defines the performance he has just completed.

John Fetzer punctuated the final performance of perhaps the last pure baseball sportsman/owner as if he had rehearsed it his entire life. It had been orchestrated down to its final detail., but the purity of its intent kept its spontaneity very much alive.

On October 10, 1983, Fetzer delivered a shocking announcement. Not only did it catch Detroit by surprise, it sent tremors throughout the entire sports world.

To the amazement of almost all, Fetzer had sold the Detroit Tigers. The announcement was not that the Tigers were about to be sold. The deal had been done. All that was left were the formalities. The club was not sold to one of the community's better known business tycoons. Instead, it went to Tom Monaghan, a relatively unknown business entrepreneur from Ann Arbor, Michigan, who turned flipping pizzas into a half-billion-dollar-a-year enterprise known as Domino's. And until the deal was announced, no one even knew the club had been for sale.

The swiftness and secrecy of the sale were beautiful. No one had suspected it. No one had a clue.

Hall of Famer George Kell succinctly put Detroit's best-kept secret into its proper perspective.

"Imagine passing ownership of a ball club with the history of the Detroit Tigers without even putting it up for sale," Kell marveled. "Mr. Fetzer was a one-of-a-kind person and his sale to Tom Monaghan proved it. You have to look at the whole picture to appreciate what all this meant.

"He refused to put the club up for sale and fish for the highest offer. There was none of this, 'I'll sell the club for this amount of money or that amount or else I'll move it to another city' sort of thing like you hear today.

"No sir. He hand-picked the person he wanted to turn the club over to. Sure, the right price meant something. Getting just the right man meant even more. That's how much he loved the Detroit Tigers. That's how much he cared for the game."

Owning the Tigers had provided Fetzer his greatest sense of pride. Although he never showed it publicly, selling the team actually fractured his heart. Ironically, the sale occurred because of his unbending commitment to the Tigers. It was a deal that had to be done in order to perpetuate the franchise in the baseball tradition in which it had been run.

"Perhaps what a lot of people will never understand is that John was the Tigers' biggest fan," explained his nephew Bruce Fetzer. "Certainly he relished his role in the behind-the-scenes operation of the industry. But above all else, he was the fiercest, most loyal Tiger fan on the face of the earth. He never had children. The Tigers became his source of pride."

Because of his uncompromising love for his team and the city, Fetzer accepted the personal heartbreak that accompanied the sale. Although he realized that his decision to sell would eventually sever him from the game that had become his life, it had to be done for the long range good of the franchise. Few understood the sacrifice Fetzer chose to make. Those who did appreciated his gentle bravery.

"I saw what had happened to the Red Sox when Tom Yawkey died," Fetzer said. "The team was passed along into an estate and a real mess occurred that affected the entire franchise. I wasn't going to let that happen to the Tigers."

The Tigers were owned by Fetzer, Inc., of which Fetzer held all but five percent of the stock, which he had permitted Jim Campbell to purchase several years prior. Late in his life, Fetzer had passed all of those shares of stock to the Fetzer Institute, which he had founded. Being a non-profit institution, it was not fiscally sound for the Institute to hold a commodity such as a baseball club.

Fetzer understood the ramifications of the situation and the sacrifice it demanded. He accepted that sacrifice, however, only after he had convinced himself that all conditions relative to perpetuating the Tiger tradition were satisfactorily guaranteed. They included:

—That the franchise was to remain in the city of Detroit.

—That the Tigers remain the symbol of Detroit's working man.

—That the franchise pass to a sole owner who was prepared to keep it operating in a fiscally sound and traditional fashion for an indefinitely long period of time.

When Fetzer hand-picked Monaghan, he was convinced the young entrepreneur could meet all stipulations. Monaghan, in fact, stated publicly that the franchise would remain in his family forever. An orderly transition was established with Fetzer serving as chairman of the board and Campbell remaining as president for at least five years.

Orderliness of transition, no doubt, significantly concerned Fetzer. But there were other outside deep concerns that had begun to chisel at Fetzer's heart. He still loved his Tigers. He still believed in all of baseball's redeeming values. But for him, the direction the game had taken was running contrary to all those beliefs which he had so fiercely defended for so many years.

"I think I seriously started to consider selling the club somewhere around 1979 or 1980," Fetzer admitted. "We were beginning to have so many problems in baseball and, at the time, I was carrying the full load. I was on every board and every committee. The player strike of 1981 brought things to a head."

Fetzer persisted. He wasn't ready to quit at that point. But disillusionment had definitely struck. Baseball had slowly changed from an institution of honor where deals were done on a handshake to the big business world of lawyers, agents and marketing strategies. Finally the game had evolved into an extension of the corporate world.

"I don't think there's any doubt that he became very much disillusioned," Kell said. "He had tried everything he could to put the game back onto an even keel. But the fun had gone out of the game."

The single incident that finally punctuated baseball's ultimate change of direction occurred at the owners' meeting in Boston in August, 1983.

It was at that meeting that Bowie Kuhn announced he was stepping down as commissioner after serving in the position since 1969. A group of dissident owners had been lobbying for his ouster. They had made it clear that they would not support the extension of Kuhn's contract once it expired at the end of the next year.

As he had hand-picked Monaghan to succeed him as owner of the Tigers, Fetzer had been instrumental in selecting Kuhn as commissioner 14 years earlier. Fetzer had done so because he felt Kuhn shared his beliefs in the traditions and honor of the game.

"Baseball had begun to tip over to the other side of the mountain," Kuhn explained, "into a dog-eat-dog kind of world. Baseball and the old traditions of honor, such as doing deals on a handshake, might be forfeited.

"It was almost a battle along those lines. Indeed, when Peter Ueberroth (the commissioner who took office in October, 1984) came along, he brought more of a commercial approach as opposed to the Judge Landis or Bowie Kuhn type of approach. I think with Peter you got a changing mood with a much more commercial style."

Sponsorship of everything from pitching changes to the seventh-inning stretch have since been introduced. In-park giveaways and gimmicks have become as common as the playing of the National Anthem before each game. The romantic technicolor of the game was changing to corporate gray. Baseball was soon to lose its last remnant of innocence.

"Disillusioned?" Kuhn mulled. "Yes. I think John clearly saw the handwriting on the wall that major changes were coming with my departure. He wanted no part of them."

Kuhn agreed to remain as commissioner through September, 30, 1984. Upon hearing the Kuhn decision not to fight for another term, Fetzer called Campbell and told him, "You better get hold of that young man from Ann Arbor ... I think it's finally time to leave."

Kuhn was made aware of Fetzer's decision.

"I have no reason to question that (my departure) tipped the scale," Kuhn said. "In fact, John flat out told me.

"John had been troubled by the way things were going anyway. But as long as I was commissioner, I think he felt the old order of honor would be preserved."

Fetzer never was prone to act on impulse. Kuhn's departure was merely the final straw. Fetzer had been troubled for some time with the changing guard of new ownership. He rejected the sentiment of trying to make money quickly at the expense of the long range good of the game.

"There were so many new owners that didn't know the difficulties of negotiating with the players union," Fetzer explained. "They (new owners) did everything they could to wreck the techniques used by the negotiating committee. They would petition for board meetings and we'd have the American and National Leagues come in and screw up the negotiations. I don't know how many times we were about to settle that strike (1981) only to have a meeting called the day before and everything got screwed up in New York. A settlement would go right out the window.

"It was a sense of frustration because of all the intense problems. And Bowie Kuhn's life was at stake. They were going to put a neophyte in there (commissioner's office) and the problems down the road in baseball were just momentous."

Fetzer knew the momentum had swung beyond maintaining the traditional structure of the game. The rules would remain the same. The objectives didn't change. But baseball was taking on a new face. To the purist, it was becoming unrecognizable.

Among the general public, particularly in Detroit, questions invariably surfaced about what would happen to the Tigers when Fetzer was no longer there. Always, however, those queries died as quickly as a weak bloop to rightfield.

Tiger fans were a peculiar brand of loyalists. At times, they grew restless with another also-ran summer. At times, they criticized Fetzer and Campbell for refusing to join the folly of frivolous free-agent spending.

For the most part, however, Tiger fans were among baseball's most forgiving. Based upon their workingman's ethic, they asked only for honesty and effort in return for their loyalty.

They were never short-changed from Fetzer or Campbell. Baseball was the sole order of business at the corner of Michigan and Trumbull. It was baseball in the traditional sense. Just like the auto plants, just like all the neighborhoods and later the suburbs that the auto industry had helped to build, the Tigers had become a staple of security. So had the notion that Fetzer would somehow always be there. So would Campbell to run the show. And with Sparky Anderson now on board as manager, it was easier than ever to forgive previous shortcomings.

Besides this sense of security, the 1983 Tigers had truly developed into one of baseball's brightest collections of young talent.

Alan Trammell and Lou Whitaker were destined to set major-league history for longevity as a shortstop/second base combination. Lance Parrish had established himself as the most explosive catcher in either league. Kirk Gibson created the definition for impact player of the '80s. Jack Morris and Dan Petry provided one of the deadliest one-two pitching punches any team had enjoyed in years. The club was pregnant with promise. And all of these youngsters had been groomed on the Tigers' farms.

The time had come, was Fetzer's low-key explanation of why he chose to sell the Tigers at the time of the announcement. It's true that he had become more interested in the enhancement of the Fetzer Institute and its pursuit of the secrets to holistic unity. But the sale also made good business sense. For more than two decades Fetzer had promised himself that he would never let the Tigers drift aimlessly in an estate situation such as the one he had encountered when he first purchased into the team.

In spite of his noble intentions, however, the very idea of selling his greatest source of pride was not easy. And that's why despite Fetzer's disappointment with the newly proclaimed direction of baseball, he still remained concerned over the Tigers' long-range stability. His insistence on keeping the Tigers in Detroit and passing his guardianship to a sole owner were a couple of self-imposed restrictions from which he refused to waver.

Still scarred from the internal battles of his long-ago syndicate ownership, Fetzer promised himself never to sell to a group of prospective buyers regardless of the price. He remained steadfast in his protection of letting the club fall into an estate entanglement similar to the one that had plagued the Briggs.

Although he never had intended them to become such an all-consuming venture, the Tigers had become a way of life for Fetzer. Once he became involved with baseball, Fetzer estimated he devoted almost 90 percent of his time to the game. Through his prominence in baseball, he came to appreciate what the franchise meant to the city and the entire state.

So given the prescribed restrictions, the once unthinkable notion of selling the Tigers now, reluctantly, was being entertained. The manner in which he carefully handed over the guardianship of the franchise would be Fetzer's last gift to the game.

Over the years, Fetzer had received numerous offers to buy the Tigers.

"Most of them came from people who couldn't even afford what it would cost to seriously examine the books," Campbell explained. "Over the years I couldn't even count how many of those came up.

"Whenever an offer came from someone of substance, I would always bring it to Mr. Fetzer."

Fetzer never seriously entertained any offer. Even at this most critical crossroads of his baseball career, Fetzer refused to publicly place the team on the market.

"I was not going to turn this franchise over to a bunch of idiots," Fetzer said. "I was not going to have some guy who has a wide ego to the point where he wants to see his name in the paper every day or wants to go out and spend wildly a lot of his fortune that he had earned elsewhere for free agents. I was not going to allow this franchise to run down the hill with so much debt that it couldn't be a viable operation. Those were the kinds of guys who were not going to own the Tigers. I wanted to find a guy who had demonstrated success as a businessman."

That "young man from Ann Arbor" was Tom Monaghan. He was an unassuming 45-year-old self-made business phenomenon. After borrowing five hundred dollars to open a pizzeria in Ypsilanti, Michigan, he turned Domino's Pizza into a half-billion dollar empire.

Monaghan's background strikingly paralleled Fetzer's. Both came from modest beginnings and borrowed money to carve out personal self-made fortunes.

Monaghan literally stepped out of the shadows of obscurity into one of the most prominent positions in professional sports. Without fanfare and almost literally overnight, he had become the owner of one of baseball's most storied franchises. And all for the mere unheard of record price of $53 million!

Fetzer's philosophy of a whisper being heard more clearly than a shout was felt around the sporting world when the sale was announced on that October Monday morning in 1983.

No one had any knowledge about the secret meetings between Fetzer and Monaghan pertaining to the sale of the club that had been going on for about six weeks. No one had a hint. Not the public. Not the players. Not the Tiger hierarchy. Not even the allegedly vigilant media, which was caught flat-footed when the deal was announced.

As Fetzer appropriately speculated, it was "probably the biggest story in the history of Detroit that broke without a leak in advance."

Fetzer insisted the deal had to be done that way. He cautioned Monaghan that if news of the sale had been leaked, the deal was dead before it was delivered. Fetzer had promised himself not to allow politics of any nature scar the integrity of the sale. The sale was founded upon the long-range stability of the Tigers. Selling the Tigers was personally traumatic enough. No undercurrent of political nonsense would be permitted to dishonor the deal.

"It had to be this way," Fetzer reasoned. "If the story had leaked, speculation in the Detroit press would have engineered all these power groups into action.

"They would have gone to City Hall. They would have gone to the Common Council. The politics would have worked overtime. They would have brought pressures to bear on the stadium and mobilizing the blacks against the whites.

"All that kind of stuff is easily done and engineered in big-city politics. And before you're through with it, they'd say, 'Why don't you sell it to a black man or to this race or to that race. Or why don't you have a balanced fringe buy it?' "

The future of the franchise for Fetzer superseded the odious element of politics. So on October 10, 1983, Fetzer announced he had sold the Tigers to Monaghan. Fetzer still would remain as chairman of the board. And Campbell would run the club as usual. Those stipulations were part of the deal and were binding for at least the next five years.

At the press conference announcing the sale, it was speculated that Monaghan had offered to keep Fetzer and Campbell to clinch the deal.

Fetzer later confessed that it was he who had made that part of the package so as to guarantee an orderly transition. Fetzer may have been selling the club, but he insisted on doing everything he could to ensure its long range stability.

The selection of Monaghan to the Fetzer throne is a story as remarkable as the silence before the sale itself. Monaghan had been devoted to the Tigers ever since his childhood. Unannounced, he traveled to spring training in Lakeland, Florida in 1982 to introduce himself to Campbell.

"I wanted to express my interest in buying the Tigers if Mr. Fetzer ever decided to sell," Monaghan said. "I believed my stepping stone to Mr. Fetzer was through Jim Campbell. I prepared myself with a lot of financial information on Domino's and tried to give him the impression that I would be the kind of owner he'd like to work for."

Campbell reported the meeting to Fetzer as he had with all other offers to purchase the club. Campbell also called University of Michigan football coach Bo Schembechler to check on his Ann Arbor neighbor. Schembechler told Campbell that Monaghan was extremely financially sound. He endorsed Monaghan's character, which also was relayed to Fetzer.

It wasn't until the following spring training that Monaghan was introduced to John Fetzer.

"I felt like I had just met with the Pope," Monaghan recalled about his first meeting.

Fetzer was impressed with Monaghan's self-made background. He also appreciated Monaghan's honesty and unashamed enthusiasm for the Tigers.

In spite of the constructive meeting, Monaghan spent almost an entire summer wondering if it had made any difference. There was no contact from Fetzer until about six weeks left in the season. It came after Fetzer had heard the news about Kuhn at the American League meeting in Boston. Fetzer called Monaghan and asked him to come to the park.

"I remember it was August 25, because it was my wedding anniversary," Monaghan said. "I apologized to my wife and remember flying down the freeway."

In the matter of the next seven weeks, the deal was structured. Although it required a battery of attorneys and accountants to construct the final product, there actually were no real negotiations.

"He asked me what the price was," Fetzer said. "I told him and he said 'O.K. That's it.'"

Monaghan admitted the $53 million price tag was more than he had imagined. But it didn't matter.

"I told him to name the price," Monaghan said. "To me, it wasn't a matter of how much because I trusted that he wouldn't take advantage of me. Buying the Tigers was something bigger than dollars and cents."

So on a crisp Monday morning before the start of the 1983 World Series between Baltimore and Philadelphia, the Tigers held a press conference that stunned the entire sporting world.

For all the cameras, Fetzer retained that singularly dignified portrait of total control. Inwardly, who really knows how he felt? This was the beginning of the end of an era. Arguably, it was the best era in the history of the Detroit franchise.

"It wasn't easy," Fetzer said. "After all, there were 27 years of sweat, blood and tears that had gone into this. But there comes a time, when for personal reasons of my own domestic situation at home, my age, and the fact that we had an owner that we felt would carry on in a solid way . . . there comes a time when you have to make a decision. And it was a tough decision."

Even after signing the papers, Fetzer couldn't escape all the temptations to second guess what he had done.

"I felt from a business standpoint that he (Monaghan) had all the qualifications and that's why I picked him," Fetzer said. "He was the only guy I ever negotiated with and that wasn't a negotiation.

"Nobody knows how a man will react once he gets into this limelight and once the press begins to take him on and he sees his name in the paper day in and day out—once he becomes an authority—once he finds they are seeking him out.

"Many, many men can't take that. They don't know how to react. They can't take it in stride. If they do lose their heads, then they're no damn good. And to that extent, the jury is still out."

The eight-and-a-half-year Monaghan era was a dichotomous mix of ecstasy and chaos. The first year after the sale, the Tigers won a club-record 104 games. They breezed through the Playoffs and the World Series. They remained competitive throughout the rest of the '80s and even won a Division title in 1987. In the early '90s, however, financial troubles struck Monaghan. In 1992, he was forced to sell the club he had vowed would stay in his family forever.

But those years were yet to unfold. The Fetzer sale that some believed never would happen actually had come to pass.

While fans welcomed Monaghan, the departure of Fetzer left an emptiness throughout the Detroit sports scene. Generations had grown up with John Fetzer's Tigers. He had established a distinct mode of operation based upon all the ideals and traditions of the game.

That emptiness pervaded the entire game of baseball. The hole remains unfilled today.

CHAPTER 18

For All Time

E very baseball fan is an expert when it comes to pick
ing favorite players. Putting together an all-time team
is one of the game's delicacies for the serious follower.
There's no way to accurately pick the ultimate all-time squad.
One man's selections might be another's folly. But certainly the
collection of stars that arose under John Fetzer's ownership of the
Tigers was formidable enough to equal those assembled by any
other owner of longevity.

Of course, these selections are subjective. But it's impossible
to question the contributions they made to the Tiger tradition. All
statistics reflect Tiger career only.

FIRST BASE—NORM CASH (1960-74) Not only was "Stormin'
Norman" one of the most feared sluggers in the American League,
he also finished his career as one of the most popular players in
Tiger history. Born in Justiceburg, Texas, Cash cast a spell over Tiger fans everywhere with his Texas drawl, impish grin and always
ready-to-play attitude. Cash never wanted to be out of the lineup.

"He was the only player I ever knew who could show up
sick, hurt, drunk, hungover or any combination of the four and still
fight to get into the lineup," said former long-time teammate Gates
Brown. "I never saw anyone like him. He had more guts than a

punch drunk fighter. You couldn't keep him down. The man wanted
to play."

Only six-feet tall and 185-pounds, Cash had a short, compact
left-handed swing that was perfectly suited for Tiger Stadium's short
rightfield porch. Sometimes Cash didn't stop at the seats. He rock-
eted four shots over the rightfield roof to lead all players in that
category. He was the first Tiger to turn the trick after Boston's Ted
Williams did it once and New York's Mickey Mantle did it three
times.

Cash recorded one of Detroit's most awesome single seasons
in 1961 when the Tigers took the pennant race into September. He
won the American League batting title with a .361 mark. He also
enjoyed career highs with 41 home runs and 132 runs batted in.
Five times in his career he belted at least 30 home runs.

He was a magician with the glove. He could scoop errant
throws from the dirt like a lizard snatching insects. He had a patent
on outrunning foul pop ups down the line and snagging them
cleanly just before they fell into the stands.

Cash was named to five All-Star teams. His enthusiasm for the
game was contagious. He made everybody laugh. No one could
help being a Norm Cash fan.

AVERAGE — .272   HR — 373   RBI — 1,087

SECOND BASE—LOU WHITAKER (1977-95) "Sweet Lou" not
only was one of the smoothest players ever to wear a Tiger uniform, he also was one of the most gifted to play the game in any era
of baseball.

Whitaker played along side of shortstop Alan Trammell his
entire career. The two set the major league record of 19 seasons
with a teammate on one team.

Whitaker to Trammell to the first baseman or Trammell to
Whitaker to first became a double-play mantra. They formed a combination upon which two generations of Tiger fans were raised.

Selected by the Tigers in the fifth round of the 1975 free agent
draft, Whitaker spent his entire major-league career in Detroit. He
retired after establishing himself as one of the game's all-around
threats. He finished high on almost every one of Detroit's all-time
leader lists. Former Manager Sparky Anderson said that Whitaker,
for his position, "had more pure talent than any other player I ever
saw."

No one turned a double play as smoothly as Whitaker. No second baseman had as strong an arm. He won three Gold Glove Awards and was voted American League Rookie of the Year for 1978 by the Baseball Writers Association of America. He was named to four All-Star teams.

At the plate, Whitaker hit for average and for power. He could deliver in the clutch almost at command. Although slight of build, Whitaker was a dangerously sneaky power hitter and finished with 244 home runs. In 1985, he pumped one over the Tiger Stadium rightfield roof.

A fan favorite throughout his career, Whitaker is expected to receive strong consideration for election into Baseball's Hall of Fame when he becomes eligible.

AVERAGE — .276   HR — 244   RBI — 1,084

SHORTSTOP—ALAN TRAMMELL (1977-96) "Tram" was the symbol of consistency for the Tigers, both on and off the field. Selected by the Tigers in the second round of the 1976 free-agent draft, Trammell also spent his entire career with Detroit.

Off the field, Trammell developed into one of the classiest pillars of the community. He never allowed his personality to change even after he established himself as a true major-league superstar.

On the field, he was the model for everything a manager looked for in a player. On defense, he made every play. Whether deep in the hole at short or up the middle behind second base, Tram rarely failed.

"The highest compliment I can give him on defense is that he made every play look routine," Anderson said. "That's really something. He never messed up the routine play. That's the sign of a great shortstop."

Tram had an arm that seemed to be controlled by a computer. He was the winner of four Gold Glove Awards. He also was named to six All-Star teams.

At the plate, Tram always delivered far more than was expected from the average shortstop. He cracked the .300 mark for a season seven times. He posted career highs of .343 with 28 home runs and 105 runs batted in while the Tigers unexpectedly won the American League East Division in 1987.

Tram made the most of his one World Series appearance, winning the Most Valuable Player Award in 1984. He led all hitters with a .450 average and nine hits, including two home runs. Once he becomes eligible, Tram is expected to receive strong consideration for election into Baseball's Hall of Fame.

AVERAGE — .285   HR — 185   RBI — 1,003

THIRD BASE—AURELIO RODRIGUEZ (1971-79) He had a vacuum cleaner for a left hand and a cannon for a right arm. In his prime, Rodriguez had few peers in the field at third base.

Rodriguez was never mistaken for impersonating a reliable hitter. What he did to enemy hitters on the left corner of the infield, however, was simply lethal.

Despite his offensive deficiencies, Rodriguez was automatically penciled into the starting lineup everyday because of his defensive magic.

He not only had range, he also had the ability to throw out a runner when it looked like he never had a chance. Many times after a diving stop, Rodriguez would rise to one knee and fire across the diamond to nip a runner by a step.

Acquired from the Washington Senators in the trade for Denny McLain, Rodriguez was the secretary of defense during the '70s. If defense could be translated to offensive statistics, Rodriguez would have been a solid .300 hitter throughout his career.

AVERAGE — .239   HR — 85   RBI — 423

RIGHTFIELD—AL KALINE (1953-74) Without question, Kaline was simply one of the best players ever in the history of the game. He spent his entire career with the Tigers.

He remains the paradigm of professional ball players. For modern times, he is the standard by which all Tiger players are measured.

Signed by the Tigers in 1953, Kaline debuted almost immediately after graduating from Baltimore's Southern High School. He never played a day in the minor leagues and spent 22 seasons with the Tigers. He was elected to Baseball's Hall of Fame on the first ballot in 1980.

There was no part of the game at which Kaline did not excel. From his remote position in rightfield, he could dictate the flow of a game. He did it with his glove and he did it with his arm.

He won ten Gold Glove Awards, including seven straight from 1961 through 1967. He was named to the All-Star team an incredible 18 times.

Offensively, Kaline was as deadly as he was in the field. He holds the major league record for the youngest player to win a batting title. He was only 20 when he captured the crown with a .340 mark in 1955. He hit 399 home runs, more than any Tiger in history. He played in 2,834 games, more than any Tiger in history. Kaline made the most of his one appearance in the World Series when he played flawlessly in the field and batted .375 in 1968.

"Al rarely said much," recalled lifelong Tiger employee Jack Tighe who actually managed Kaline in 1957. "He did it all on the field. He never made it look flashy. He made everything look routine. He made it look so easy, you kind of took him for granted. That's how great he was."

Kaline capped his Hall of Fame career in 1974 when he collected the 3,000th hit of his career. He finished with 3,007.

Kaline did it quietly. He did it with class. He will, for many years, be remembered as modern baseball's best Tiger ever.

AVERAGE — .297   HR — 399   RBI — 1,583

CENTERFIELD—MICKEY STANLEY (1964-78) At best, Stanley was a very average major league hitter. On defense, however, he arguably was the best centerfielder the Tigers ever had.

Signed by the Tigers out of Grand Rapids, Michigan, prior to the free-agent draft, Stanley was an athlete in the true sense of the word. He wasn't fast, but he was athletically quick. He had an instinct for the game that gave him a couple of extra steps to make up for his lack of blinding speed.

Playing in Tiger Stadium, which features the largest centerfield in the majors, Stanley caught up to balls which many outfielders gave up on. He played without fear. He crashed into fences like professional wrestlers use the ring ropes. For his defensive excellence, Stanley earned four Gold Glove Awards.

Stanley won his first Gold Glove in 1968. For the World Series that fall, he switched to shortstop in one of the most stunning moves in Series history.

"He never questioned the move," said former General Manager Jim Campbell. "There was a lot of pressure on him and he could have embarrassed himself. But Mickey knew how much he could help the team. That showed me what kind of man he was."

Stanley spent his entire career with the Tigers and set the standard for all future Tiger centerfielders.

AVERAGE — .248   HR — 117   RBI — 500

LEFTFIELD—WILLIE HORTON (1963-77) Horton remains the portrait of the punishing power hitter. For the Tigers and their tradition, he was much, much more.

Raised only a mile from Tiger Stadium, Horton was signed by his hometown team and turned a dream into real-life history. He resembled a heavyweight boxer more than a ball player. On the diamond, there wasn't much he couldn't do.

Signed out of Northwestern High School prior to the free agent draft, Horton spent parts of three seasons in the minor leagues before exploding onto the American League scene.

Horton was known for his prodigious power to every part of the ball park. Six times for the Tigers he cracked at least 25 home runs. When the Tigers won the World Series in 1968, Horton led the offense during the regular season with 36 homers.

While he will be remembered most for those majestically long home runs, he also was a deceivingly good outfielder. He had an instinct for knowing which balls to gamble on and which ones to play safe.

One of his most memorable defensive gems came in the 1968 World Series when he threw Lou Brock out at the plate in a controversial play in which the Cardinal failed to slide.

Horton became Detroit's first black superstar. He may not have liked it, but Horton was turned into a symbol for the inner city black. He was the kind of person, however, who never measured anything by color. All he ever wanted to do was to play ball for the Tigers. And he did so in a style that will never be forgotten.

AVERAGE — .276   HR — 262   RBI — 886

CATCHER—BILL FREEHAN (1961-76) Freehan was another local talent upon which the Tigers capitalized. Signed off the campus of the University of Michigan prior to the free-agent draft, the all-around athlete spent his entire career with the Tigers.

During Fetzer's years as owner, he also was blessed with another standout catcher in Lance Parrish who was drafted by Detroit in 1974. Freehan, however, was the model of longevity and excellence at one of the most demanding positions on the field.

Freehan was a master at controlling a game. He handled his pitchers like a weather-worn cowboy breaks a horse. He won five straight Gold Glove Awards from 1965 through 1969.

The All-Star Game became an annual stop of Freehan's summers. From 1964 through 1973 he was named to the team each year. He also was selected to the 1975 squad. He finished his career with 11 All-Star selections, second in Tiger history to Kaline's 18 calls.

Offensively, Freehan contributed more than the average catcher. He finished with a .262 average, 200 home runs and 758 runs batted in. It was behind the plate, though, where Freehan was the master. For most of his career, he had few peers.

AVERAGE — .262   HR — 200   RBI — 758

RIGHT-HAND STARTER—JACK MORRIS (1977-90)   What Morris may have lacked in ability, he more than compensated for with determination. And there wasn't much in ability that the Minnesota native didn't have.

Morris had a mean streak once he reached the mound. It was the kind of streak that refused to let him quit until the game was over, regardless who finished on top.

Selected by the Tigers in the fifth round of the 1976 free-agent draft, Morris became one of the franchise's most prolific starters. Once he worked his way into the starting rotation, he rarely missed a turn.

Twice he won at least 20 games for the Tigers. He finished with a 198-150 won-lost record. He made 408 starts for Detroit. Except for Mickey Lolich with 459, no other pitcher in history made more for the Tigers.

Morris was a bulldog who always pitched better when the pressure was on. He posted two complete-game victories in the 1984 World Series.

"He was as bull-headed as they come," Manager Sparky Anderson said. "That's the way all great ones are. You couldn't take him out of a game. He'd fight you all the way.

"Jack was an athlete in the true sense of the word. He could run in the outfield all day long. If he hadn't been a pitcher, he could have made it as an outfielder or infielder. If there was a big game to win, you wanted him to have the ball. He was one of the fiercest competitors I've ever been around."

STARTS — 408   WINS — 198   LOSSES — 150

LEFT-HAND STARTER—MICKEY LOLICH (1963-75) He looked more like those assembly line auto workers he performed in front of than one of the most reliable lefties in the history of the game. Without a question, though, Lolich was a manager's best friend.

That's because he always wanted the baseball. Once he took it, no one could get it out of his hand.

During his 13-year career in Detroit, the likable lefty with the neighborly potbelly missed just one start. He was the savior of the bullpen and a manager's best insurance policy.

Lolich won 25 games in 1971. He followed that with 22 the next year. Yet he was rarely dazzling; he simply was more consistent than rain showers in Seattle.

Lolich was signed by the Tigers before the free-agent draft. From 1964 through 1974, he won at least 14 games a year. Even more amazing than his consistency, however, was the durability of that beautiful left arm.

Once he broke into the starting rotation in 1964, he never pitched less than 200 innings. From 1971 through 1974, he had a string of 376, 327, 309 and 308 innings pitched.

The man simply did not know how to quit.

No other pitcher in the history of the Tigers made more starts than his 459. He had 190 complete games and finished as the club's third all-time winner with 207 victories. He is the all-time Tiger leader in strikeouts with 2,679.

Lolich won three starts in the 1968 World Series when he was named Most Valuable Player. No Tiger fan will forget the frozen image of Freehan and Lolich hugging at the end of Game 7.

No one will forget No. 29 going out to the mound over and over again.

STARTS — 459   WINS — 207   LOSSES — 175

RELIEF PITCHER—JOHN HILLER (1965-80) Nicknamed "Ratso" because of his physical resemblance to Ratso Rizzo, the character played by Dustin Hoffman in the movie *Midnight Cow-*

boy, Hiller had the perfect make-up for the short relief man.

He was fearless and could bounce back from adversity better than a cat who had all nine lives left.

It wasn't that Hiller didn't care about what happened on the field. He just eventually realized that what happened off the field was what mattered most in life.

Hiller was just another faceless mediocre pitcher the first half of his career. It was only after the heart attack he suffered that forced him to sit out the 1971 season and half of 1972 that he changed his outlook on life.

Hiller was moved to the bullpen exclusively in 1973. He responded with a 10-5 record and a then American League record 38 saves. It was the comeback heard around the nation. He followed that with a few more solid years during Detroit's rebuilding project.

Born and raised in Canada, Hiller was signed by the Tigers prior to the free-agent draft. He spent his entire career in Detroit and leads all Tiger pitchers with 545 appearances. He finished second on the club's all-time save list with 125.

With the game on the line, few pitchers were as fearless as Hiller. In the clubhouse, he became the most positive influence on young players and veterans alike.

WINS — 87   LOSSES — 76   SAVES — 125

There are arguments for other players. Certainly, the Tigers have had their share of good ones. Under Fetzer's reign, however, this assembly could take the field with an all-time squad from any other club.

If you went to war with this group, you would be sure to win your share of battles.

CHAPTER 19

The Men in the Dugout

J ack Tighe was John Fetzer's first Tiger manager. Sparky Anderson was his last.

Although a quarter-century apart, both sound like the same person when describing why managing the Detroit Tigers under Fetzer and General Manager Jim Campbell was the best job in baseball.

"I don't mean to make this sound blasphemous, because Mr. Fetzer never looked at it this way," Tighe said. "But working for him was like a good person working for God. He didn't want any bad people around him.

"Managing the Tigers under him was the best job in baseball, barring none. And that includes the Yankees. The manager had one man to report to—Jim Campbell. And Campbell had one man to report to—Mr. Fetzer. That's simple. That's how baseball is supposed to be."

Anderson enjoyed the longest managerial tenure under Fetzer. He was named manager on June 12, 1979, and stayed through the 1995 season. Although Fetzer officially sold the club on October 10, 1983, he maintained an interest in the franchise and remained as chairman of the board for the next five years.

"The days of owners like Mr. Fetzer and bosses like Jim Campbell are over in baseball," Anderson said. "Mr. Fetzer owned the club because he loved baseball so much. He wanted to make the whole game—not just the Tigers—better. He didn't need the club to make money. He had all the money in the world.

"Owners like Mr. Fetzer and Tom Yawkey and John Galbreath and Calvin Griffith and Walter and Peter O'Malley are never going to come around again. Baseball is corporate now. The corporations are in it for the money. And they want their money right away. The owners run their teams just like they run their corporations. It's not a club anymore."

Anderson concurs with Tighe's analysis of the benefits of a manager reporting to just one boss.

"In all my years of working for Mr. Fetzer and Jim Campbell, I never was bothered once on any baseball matter," Anderson said. "When those two guys hired you to do a job, they expected you to do it. They didn't stand around second guessing you on every move you made. They stepped out of the way and let you get to work.

"That's the way the good teams did it in baseball. That's the only way to get a job done. I ain't saying that all of today's owners go around meddling in the manager's business. But I do know that things are different now. You never had to worry with Mr. Fetzer and Jim Campbell. And you never had to wonder if they would back you up when the going got tough. They were there every step of the way. If you needed any help, all you had to do was ask."

The hands-off approach is a giant step toward baseball efficiency. But it can only work in conjunction with two specific elements. First, the owner must have the proper personnel in all the right positions. Secondly, the owner must have the courage to do the right thing and never waver in the face of sometimes unjustified criticism.

With Campbell in place as the general manager at the end of the 1962 season, Fetzer felt comfortable that the club could stick to its program of developing winning teams from within its own system. And at all costs, he left the manager alone.

Fetzer headed a syndicate that purchased the Tigers in July, 1956. But the group did not officially take over until after the season. From 1957 until finally stepping down in 1988, Fetzer had eleven managers serve under him. Considering the normal turnover in this unusually volatile position, the number is staggeringly low. Two deaths and two mid-season dismissals also called for four interim managers.

Chronologically, from when Fetzer entered the Tiger family, these were the men who led the teams on the field. All statistics reflect Tiger records only.

JACK TIGHE (1957-58) Tighe was the classic organization man. He first joined the Tigers as a catcher for the Charleston, West Virginia, minor league team in 1935.

As with so many managers, Tighe discovered quickly that his playing ability wouldn't get him further than a bloop to the outfield in baseball. In 1940, he embarked on his managerial career with the Tigers' team in Muskegon, Michigan.

He bounced around a variety of spots, including Buffalo, New York. It was there that he was a roommate of Jim Campbell who later would serve as the Tiger boss for three decades. At the time, Campbell was Buffalo's business manager.

Tighe was the typical, old style, no-nonsense field boss. He was brought in to provide a "get-tough" attitude. Tighe promised that his players no longer would perform "like contented turtles." He wanted emotion and hustle.

Tighe had a terrific sense of humor and answered all questions with disarming honesty in old fashioned baseball style. Because of his candor and a gift for being able to laugh during the toughest times, he was always a favorite with the media.

Kenyon Brown was one member of the syndicate that purchased the Tigers in mid-1956. He once told Tighe that it looked like he was having some trouble with the Tigers.

"You'd have trouble, too, if you had to manage this cast of characters everyday," Tighe retorted.

Tighe was elevated to the Tiger job for the start of the 1957 season. The Tigers finished 78-76 that season. After 49 games with a 21-28 mark the following year, Tighe was relieved of his duties.

Tighe was considered to have few peers when judging baseball talent and the internal make-up of a player. More importantly, he demonstrated uncontested loyalty to the organization. He later served the Tigers as a special assignment scout. Except for a four-year stint with the Milwaukee Braves, Tighe spent his entire career, spanning 54 years, in the Tiger organization. He was relieved of his duties shortly after Mike Ilitch purchased the Tigers in 1992.

Year	W	L	Pct.	Place
1957	78	76	.506	4
1958	21	28	.429	5
Total	99	104	.488	

BILL NORMAN (1958-59) At the time, the Tigers felt they had to go outside of the organization. The ownership syndicate was still new to baseball and was restless to see immediate improvement in the standings. They looked for a manager who might be easier on the players.

Norman had managed in the minor leagues. The year with the Tigers was his only major league managerial stop. Norman had appeared in a total of 37 games as an outfielder for the Chicago White Sox in 1931-32.

Norman's style of managing was to throw the ball out on to the field and let the players play. He wanted to remain in the big leagues and therefore tried to ingratiate himself with the media, the players and John McHale who was in charge of player personnel.

The politics of a syndicate ownership and a 2-15 start in 1959 caught up with Norman quickly. It was Norman who labeled the Tiger syndicate as "The Twelve Apostles."

When informed that the syndicate was comprised of 11 members, he quickly retorted: "Yeah, but one of them always brings his wife to the meetings."

Year	W	L	Pct.	Place
1958	56	49	.533	5
1959	2	15	.118	8
Total	58	64	.475	

JIMMIE DYKES (1959-60) Considered by most baseball experts as a man with outstanding baseball insight, Dykes managed in the major leagues for 21 seasons. He was near the end of his career when he came to Detroit. He managed the Tigers for just two years.

Dykes was half of one of the most bizarre moves in baseball history. In the middle of the 1960 season, Tiger President Bill DeWitt traded Dykes to Cleveland for Indians Manager Joe Gordon.

Before joining the Tigers, Dykes managed the White Sox from 1934 into 1946. He later managed the Philadelphia Phillies, the Baltimore Orioles and Cincinnati Reds before joining the Tigers and then finished with the Indians.

Dykes was easy going and believed in treating players as men. When asked about what rules he would have for the players, he responded, "Why have any rules? Nobody is going to pay attention to them."

Year	W	L	Pct.	Standing
1959	74	63	.540	4
1960	44	52	.458	6
Total	118	115	.506	

JOE GORDON (1960) It didn't take Gordon long to smell out the problems that had arisen from an 11-man ownership. Especially one that was involved with the trading of managers. Before DeWitt could fire Gordon after the 1960 season, Gordon resigned from his position.

Gordon had a reputation for being a knowledgeable manager, but one who crossed the line of partying with the players.

Gordon was finishing his third year as the Cleveland manager before his stunning trade. He managed the Kansas City Athletics in 1961 and again in 1969.

Year	W	L	Pct.	Standing
1960	26	31	.456	6

BOB SCHEFFING (1961-63) Scheffing was credited by some baseball experts as possessing one of the sharpest minds the Tigers ever had. By everyone, he was considered to be one of the classiest persons that anyone had met.

Scheffing was an outstanding communicator, particularly with young players. He demonstrated that quality in his first year with the Tigers as he took the 1961 team on an unexpected pennant run that had the whole community rocking.

The Tigers were just starting to bring up some of the bright young talent they had maturing in their farm system. Few expected them to make a run for the pennant this soon. But behind a combination of veterans and youngsters, Scheffing took them all the way into a Labor Day showdown with the Yankees before finally settling for second place.

The Tigers tied their then-club record of 101 wins behind Scheffing. But the young talent was still too inconsistent to make an annual run for the flag.

Scheffing made it through the first 60 games of the 1963 season before being relieved of his duties. He had impressed Fetzer so much with his class that Scheffing shared the radio broadcast duties for the 1964 season.

Year	W	L	Pct.	Standing
1961	101	61	.623	2
1962	85	76	.528	4
1963	24	36	.400	9
Total	210	173	.548	

CHARLIE DRESSEN (1963-65) Dressen came to the Tigers as one of the most celebrated managers in the game. He brought class and a history to Detroit. He was brought in to liven up the Tigers and help the promising batch of youngsters mature.

Dressen had managed 12 years in the big leagues before coming to Detroit. He had managed the Brooklyn Dodgers in the World Series of 1952 and 1953. Dressen was always full of life and made all those around him feel as good as he did.

"He knew the game," Tighe said. "He had a real knack for picking out all the trouble makers real fast. Then he'd get rid of them. For a short period of time, he might have been the best manager the Tigers had."

It was a short period. Too short.

In 1965, when the gold mine of young Tiger talent was really starting to develop, Dressen suffered a heart attack and had to leave the team in the middle of the season. He returned in 1966 only to suffer another attack. He died on August 10th.

During his absence in 1965 and again in 1966, he was replaced on an interim basis by Coach Bob Swift. In an eerie set of circumstances, however, Swift was forced to leave the team during the 1966 season after a spot was detected on his lung. He was replaced by Coach Frank Skaff. Swift died on October 17.

Had Dressen been healthy, it could have been he who led the Tigers to their glorious World Championship season of 1968. But fate was too strong even for jolly Charlie Dressen.

Year	W	L	Pct.	Standing
1963	55	47	.539	5
1964	85	77	.525	4
1965	65	55	.542	3
1966	16	10	.615	3
Total	221	189	.539	

MAYO SMITH (1967-70) It seems ironic that a man named "Smith" should take the Tigers to their greatest glory since their World Championship of 1945. But this man named Smith was the man in the right place at the right time.

Smith was the recipient of the mother lode of young Tiger talent. He was smart enough to throw the ball on to the field and then get out of the way.

Smith had never finished higher than fourth in managerial stops with the Philadelphia Phillies and Cincinnati Reds before coming to Detroit. But he realized his own managerial maturation process in 1967 when the Tigers got involved in the tightest pennant race in the history of the American League.

The Tigers split a doubleheader with California on the last day of the season and finished in a second-place tie behind Boston.

In 1968, it was all Detroit, as the Tigers charged to the pennant and then rallied to beat the Cardinals in seven games for the World Championship.

Smith deserves credit for the stunning switch of Mickey Stanley from centerfield to shortstop for the World Series. Smith had to devise a way to get Al Kaline's bat into the lineup.

The Tigers slipped to second in 1969 and fourth in 1970. Toward the end of the 1970 season, Smith knew his fate had been sealed. For the good of the team a change had to be made.

Year	W	L	Pct.	Standing
1967	91	71	.562	T-2
1968	103	59	.636	1
1969	90	72	.556	2
1970	79	83	.488	4
Total	363	285	.560	

BILLY MARTIN (1971-73) It was not the proverbial match made in heaven. It looked like Jack Nicholson landing the lead in *The Sound of Music.*

There were some good times. In the end, however, the Fetzer-Martin combination proved to screech toward its almost inevitable chaotic finale.

For a couple of years, the unlikely coupling was more disruptive to American League foes than it was to the Tigers, who found their way back into the Playoffs.

The Tigers needed a jolt to lift them from the lethargy they had fallen into under Smith. What better way than with the volcanic Billy Martin?

"We get along all right," Fetzer said during Martin's tenure. "We just know what Billy is. Let it go in one ear and out the other. He's had a lot to learn as an inexperienced kid and he doesn't learn easily. He doesn't take orders easily, but we're living with him and he's learning a lot at our expense. He's got a good fan appeal, and he's got a good faculty for getting production out of the older guys, which a lot of managers can't do."

After a second-place finish in 1971, Martin and the Tigers scratched their way into the 1972 Playoffs against the powerful Oakland Athletics. The Tigers took it to the final game before all the clawing, jabbing, spitting and poking of Martin's scrappy gang finally ran out.

Again in 1973, the Tigers slipped into first place in early August. The clock had been ticking on Martin, though. Finally, those long-ago predicted off-field escapades sounded the alarm against him. A series of violations of club and league regulations left the club no choice but to dismiss the fiery manager.

The indiscretions by Martin caused embarrassment to the club and also to the game. Fetzer wanted nothing more than another

World Championship for the city. But never at the expense of baseball's image.

As with every team he managed, Martin left town with the reputation of being an outstanding strategist between the foul lines. It was after he left the park that the real problems began. Martin was fired in September and replaced by interim Manager Joe Schultz for the rest of the season.

Year	W	L	Pct.	Standing
1971	91	71	.562	2
1972	86	70	.551	1
1973	85	77	.525	3
Total	262	218	.546	

RALPH HOUK (1974-78) Houk came to the Tigers with all the glitter of the Yankees and a reputation for being one of the finest managers in the game.

His job with the Tigers was the role of the fall guy. He knew it coming in. He did the job bravely and then turned over a team that was on the verge of becoming a winner.

Houk was charged with leading a massive rebuilding program as the Tigers began to dismantle their long-time winning machine while starting work on another.

It wasn't easy for someone who not only had played for the Yankees in their glory days, but also managed them for 11 years. But Houk knew what was expected of him. He performed his job with all the grace that Fetzer and Campbell had expected.

Fetzer wanted to return a touch of class to the Tigers. He picked the right person with the man known as "The Major" for his World War II heroics.

"Ralph knew he was in for a beating when he took the job," Campbell said. "We were rebuilding and needed a strong leader. I can't thank Ralph enough for the way he handled himself and the team. He helped get us back on the right track."

In his first two years, the Tigers finished last. The 1975 team suffered through a 19-game losing streak. In 1976, the Tigers and baseball were blessed by Mark "The Bird" Fidrych. By the time Houk left, the Tigers were starting to develop such youngsters as Alan Trammell and Lou Whitaker.

Year	W	L	Pct.	Standing
1974	72	90	.444	6
1975	57	102	.358	6
1976	74	87	.460	5
1977	74	88	.457	4
1978	86	76	.531	5
Total	363	443	.450	

LES MOSS (1979) With the coming of several promising youngsters through their minor-league system, the Tigers promoted Moss from their Class AAA affiliate at Evansville. Moss was a former catcher and is credited with arming Lance Parrish with the basics of his position.

It's impossible to determine how good Moss may have been. He was replaced after 53 games by the legendary Sparky Anderson.

It hurt Campbell to replace the soft-spoken professional. Moss was offered another position in the organization. But Campbell explained that he could not take the chance of letting Anderson slip by. About a half-dozen other clubs were trying to lure the white-haired wonder back into the game when Campbell claimed him for Detroit.

The announcement of Anderson's hiring occurred on June 12. Coach Dick Tracewski served as interim manager for two games until Anderson was able to report. The Tigers won both.

Year	W	L	Pct.	Standing
1979	27	26	.509	5

SPARKY ANDERSON (1979-95) Men such as Fetzer ordinarily remain neutral about expressing favorites on their clubs. Anything pertaining to Sparky, however, can hardly remain neutral.

"For a variety of individual reasons, I respected every manager that served the Tigers," Fetzer said. "But I have to admit that Sparky was my favorite. He's a very special person that embodies everything that is good about the game."

Sparky not only embodied baseball's charm, he also radiated the class and sensitive human qualities that Fetzer valued so highly.

Sparky promptly demonstrated why he is Sparky on his first day in Detroit. He promised a championship within his first five years. And also vintage Sparky, the Tigers delivered in 1984.

By the time Sparky left the Tigers after the 1995 season, he had rewritten the record books. With 1,331 victories, Sparky leads all Tiger managers in franchise history. With 2,194 for his career, only Connie Mack and John McGraw have more than Sparky in the history of the game.

"I had to be the luckiest man on the face of the earth to get the job working for Mr. Fetzer and Jim Campbell," Sparky said. "These were two real baseball men. They understood the game and all the things it took to win a championship and win it with class.

"I remember talking to Ralph Houk years ago when the Tigers were struggling. He told me if I ever had the chance to manage the Tigers, don't pass it up. I thanked him for that piece of advice later."

Year	W	L	Pct.	Standing
1979	56	50	.528	5
1980	84	78	.519	5
1981	60	49	.550	4
1982	83	79	.512	4
1983	92	70	.568	2
1984	104	58	.642	1
1985	84	77	.522	3
1986	87	75	.537	3
1987	98	64	.605	1
1988	88	74	.543	2
1989	59	103	.364	7
1990	79	83	.488	3
1991	84	78	.519	T-2
1992	75	87	.463	6
1993	85	77	.525	T-3
1994	53	62	.461	5
1995	60	84	.417	4
Total	1331	1248	.516	

Fetzer was blessed with a variety of competent managers, each with their particular strengths.

The best was saved for last for Fetzer. It seems appropriate since he and Sparky shared a near-religious reverence for the spirit of baseball.

CHAPTER 20

Tradition

S parky Anderson always was quick to answer a reporter when asked how baseball would survive his departure. "Babe Ruth died in 1948, right?" the white-haired former Tiger manager would rhetorically ask. "And we're still playing baseball today. That's how the game will survive. It will always survive because it's bigger than any one person."

John Fetzer died on February 20, 1991. And, of course, baseball survives. It will continue to survive the passing of all the great figures—both present and future.

Its survival, however, continues down the path that led to Fetzer's decision to leave the game in the first place. By the time of passing of the present generation, only a fool would predict where that path may lead.

Baseball points proudly to record attendance figures. The numbers are indisputable. For that increase, however, baseball has paid an exacting price. So much so, that the game has subtly shifted its appeal from a sport of the working class to an event for the corporate elite.

The sales pitch of luxury suites has muffled the chatter of the Hot Stove League. Cries for publicly funded construction of ultra-modern stadiums are followed by owners' threats of moving the franchise if petitions go unheeded. Marketing gimmicks are designed to cover baseball mediocrity so as not to squash potential revenues from advertisers and upscale customers.

Baseball's financial revolution forced these inevitable changes. It hasn't made the game bad. It hasn't strangled its inherent goodness.

It has, however, created a vacuum for the purist who came from the era when baseball served as the unofficial sporting conscience for the nation. It was an era when baseball resisted the trappings of corporate big business far longer than any other sport. It was an era during which fans took great comfort with getting lost in their devotion to baseball.

While Fetzer ferociously protected his anonymity, he was even more devout with his protection of baseball's spirit. He never wavered in his belief that baseball belonged to the working man. He never was afraid to defend that belief against what ultimately became overwhelming odds.

Fetzer needs no romantic eulogy. He wouldn't have wanted one. His record has been historically documented. It confirms that he believed in baseball's simple qualities. And he fervently fought to maintain the traditions upon which the game was built.

Fetzer remained an optimist throughout his life. He did not leave the game bitterly. He left it disillusioned.

His passing brought to an end the colorful era of baseball's sportsman/owner. With that passing went the days of a hushed exuberance. They have been replaced by hyper hard-sell governed by the rules of contemporary corporate America.

Lost in the evolution are the days when deals were done on a handshake. Before he finally stepped away from the game, Fetzer was well aware of the irreversible changes.

"He clearly saw the handwriting on the wall," said former Baseball Commissioner Bowie Kuhn. "He saw the changes that were coming and he wanted no part of them."

Any historical figure is necessarily measured by the legacy he leaves. Did that figure make a difference during the time of his participation? Did his influence create a change over the way things were?

From a tangible standpoint, Fetzer made a significant difference in baseball. He made a difference in Detroit and an even greater difference in the overall game.

For Detroit:

—He transformed the Tigers into one of the most respected franchises in professional sports.

—He continually provided Detroit with a competitive team developed from the baseball tradition of building from within.

—He kept the Tigers in the City of Detroit.

—He kept ticket prices at levels within the reach of the average working man.

—When he decided it was finally time to leave, he turned over a debt-free franchise on the brink of a World Championship. The economic stability of the franchise guaranteed the team would remain in Detroit long after Fetzer was gone.

For baseball, his significance was even more widely felt:

—He created a network television package whereby all teams share equally in the revenues.

—He served in positions of leadership on baseball's highest governing councils.

—He served as unofficial adviser and confidant to franchise owners from both leagues.

But it was his intangible contributions that are much more significant. They are difficult to depict, but far more defining of the man.

Throughout his life in baseball, Fetzer was unashamed to express his passion for tradition. He was a willing volunteer in the fight to keep that tradition alive.

That inherent spirit of baseball survives today. But it is forced to breathe sporadically under several layers of corporate clutter.

"Let me put it this way," Kuhn said. "John Fetzer would fit today in the sense that baseball needs his wisdom and compassion. But I don't think he would tolerate what's going on in the game today."

From the turn of the century when baseball began its climb to its position of prominence on the American conscience, the game has endured its share of problems. No single part of American society escapes the doubts and downfalls of everyday life.

There was a time, though, and not so long ago, when life at least appeared to be a whole lot less complicated. Baseball, in its own small way, helped to provide that simple sense of security.

And it was men like John Fetzer who kept that tradition alive. Forever gone are the days when deals were done on a handshake.